OPPOSING
VIEWPOINTS®
SERIES

The Internet

Other Books of Related Interest:

Opposing Viewpoints Series
Internet Censorship

Mass Media

Netiquette and Online Ethics

At Issue Series
Are Social Networking Sites Harmful?

Cell Phones in Schools

Location-Based Social Networking and Services

Sexting

Current Controversies Series
Mobile Apps

E-books

Internet Activism

"Congress shall make
no law . . . abridging
the freedom of speech,
or of the press."

First Amendment to the US Constitution

The basic foundation of our democracy is the First Amendment guarantee of freedom of expression. The Opposing Viewpoints series is dedicated to the concept of this basic freedom and the idea that it is more important to practice it than to enshrine it.

OPPOSING VIEWPOINTS® SERIES

The Internet

Jack Lasky, Book Editor

GREENHAVEN PRESS
A part of Gale, Cengage Learning

GALE
CENGAGE Learning·

Farmington Hills, Mich • San Francisco • New York • Waterville, Maine
Meriden, Conn • Mason, Ohio • Chicago

GALE
CENGAGE Learning

Judy Galens, *Manager, Frontlist Acquisitions*

© 2016 Greenhaven Press, a part of Gale, Cengage Learning.

Gale and Greenhaven Press are registered trademarks used herein under license.

For more information, contact:
Greenhaven Press
27500 Drake Rd.
Farmington Hills, MI 48331-3535
Or you can visit our Internet site at gale.cengage.com

For product information and technology assistance, contact us at

Gale Customer Support, 1-800-877-4253
For permission to use material from this text or product, submit all requests online at www.cengage.com/permissions

Further permissions questions can be emailed to permissionrequest@cengage.com

Articles in Greenhaven Press anthologies are often edited for length to meet page requirements. In addition, original titles of these works are changed to clearly present the main thesis and to explicitly indicate the author's opinion. Every effort is made to ensure that Greenhaven Press accurately reflects the original intent of the authors. Every effort has been made to trace the owners of copyrighted material.

Cover Image copyright © My Life Graphic/Shutterstock.com.

LIBRARY OF CONGRESS CATALOGING-IN-PUBLICATION DATA

Internet (Greenhaven Press)
  The Internet / Jack Lasky, Book Editor.
    pages cm. -- (Opposing viewpoints)
  Includes bibliographical references and index.
  ISBN 978-0-7377-7554-9 (hardcover) -- ISBN 978-0-7377-7555-6 (pbk.)
  1. Internet access. 2. Internet governance. 3. Internet. I. Lasky, Jack. II. Title.
  TK5105.8855.I58 2016
  004.67'8--dc23
                        2015022316

Printed in the United States of America
1 2 3 4 5   19 18 17 16 15

Contents

Chapter 1: How Should the Internet Be Governed?

Chapter 2: How Does the Internet Impact the World?

Chapter 3: What Challenges Does the Internet Pose?

Chapter 4: Can the Internet Be Dangerous?

Why Consider Opposing Viewpoints?

> *"The only way in which a human being can make some approach to knowing the whole of a subject is by hearing what can be said about it by persons of every variety of opinion and studying all modes in which it can be looked at by every character of mind. No wise man ever acquired his wisdom in any mode but this."*
>
> John Stuart Mill

In our media-intensive culture it is not difficult to find differing opinions. Thousands of newspapers and magazines and dozens of radio and television talk shows resound with differing points of view. The difficulty lies in deciding which opinion to agree with and which "experts" seem the most credible. The more inundated we become with differing opinions and claims, the more essential it is to hone critical reading and thinking skills to evaluate these ideas. Opposing Viewpoints books address this problem directly by presenting stimulating debates that can be used to enhance and teach these skills. The varied opinions contained in each book examine many different aspects of a single issue. While examining these conveniently edited opposing views, readers can develop critical thinking skills such as the ability to compare and contrast authors' credibility, facts, argumentation styles, use of persuasive techniques, and other stylistic tools. In short, the Opposing Viewpoints Series is an ideal way to attain the higher-level thinking and reading skills so essential in a culture of diverse and contradictory opinions.

In addition to providing a tool for critical thinking, Opposing Viewpoints books challenge readers to question their own strongly held opinions and assumptions. Most people form their opinions on the basis of upbringing, peer pressure, and personal, cultural, or professional bias. By reading carefully balanced opposing views, readers must directly confront new ideas as well as the opinions of those with whom they disagree. This is not to argue simplistically that everyone who reads opposing views will—or should—change his or her opinion. Instead, the series enhances readers' understanding of their own views by encouraging confrontation with opposing ideas. Careful examination of others' views can lead to the readers' understanding of the logical inconsistencies in their own opinions, perspective on why they hold an opinion, and the consideration of the possibility that their opinion requires further evaluation.

Evaluating Other Opinions

To ensure that this type of examination occurs, Opposing Viewpoints books present all types of opinions. Prominent spokespeople on different sides of each issue as well as well-known professionals from many disciplines challenge the reader. An additional goal of the series is to provide a forum for other, less known, or even unpopular viewpoints. The opinion of an ordinary person who has had to make the decision to cut off life support from a terminally ill relative, for example, may be just as valuable and provide just as much insight as a medical ethicist's professional opinion. The editors have two additional purposes in including these less known views. One, the editors encourage readers to respect others' opinions—even when not enhanced by professional credibility. It is only by reading or listening to and objectively evaluating others' ideas that one can determine whether they are worthy of consideration. Two, the inclusion of such viewpoints encourages the important critical thinking skill of objectively evaluating an author's credentials and bias. This evaluation will illuminate an author's reasons for taking a particular stance on an issue and will aid in readers' evaluation of the author's ideas.

It is our hope that these books will give readers a deeper understanding of the issues debated and an appreciation of the complexity of even seemingly simple issues when good and honest people disagree. This awareness is particularly important in a democratic society such as ours in which people enter into public debate to determine the common good. Those with whom one disagrees should not be regarded as enemies but rather as people whose views deserve careful examination and may shed light on one's own.

Thomas Jefferson once said that "difference of opinion leads to inquiry, and inquiry to truth." Jefferson, a broadly educated man, argued that "if a nation expects to be ignorant and free . . . it expects what never was and never will be." As individuals and as a nation, it is imperative that we consider the opinions of others and examine them with skill and discernment. The Opposing Viewpoints series is intended to help readers achieve this goal.

David L. Bender and Bruno Leone,
Founders

Introduction

*"The speed and scope of the transforma-
tion of our communication environment
by Internet and wireless communication
has triggered all kind of utopian and
dystopian perceptions around the world.
As in all moments of major technological change, people, companies, and institutions feel the depth of the change, but
they are often overwhelmed by it, out of
sheer ignorance of its effects."*

—Manuel Castells,
*"The Impact of the Internet on Society:
A Global Perspective,"* September 8, 2014

There has been perhaps no technological innovation that has had a greater impact on society than the Internet. Since it was first devised, the Internet has grown and evolved to be a veritably ubiquitous entity that affects virtually every aspect of modern life in some way. As a communication medium and an invaluable tool for everything from commerce to education and beyond, the Internet has irrevocably changed the way people interact with one another and the world at large. Indeed, the Internet has shaped the very face of the modern world, creating a global community that is more closely connected than ever before.

The historical roots of the Internet can be traced back to the 1960s, when it was first created in US military computer laboratories. At the time, the US Department of Defense (DOD) was deeply entrenched in the Cold War and preparing for what seemed to be the very real possibility of nuclear hostilities with the Soviet Union. As part of its efforts to ensure that the United States was fully prepared to cope with a nuclear attack, the DOD sought, among other things, to create a backup communication network that could be used if traditional means of communication were disrupted for a prolonged period. The responsibility of devising and activating this new communication network fell to the DOD's Advanced Research Projects Agency (ARPA). As such, its subsequent invention was referred to as ARPANET.

ARPANET was an experimental computer network designed to allow computers in different locations to connect with each other through a packet-switched network. Packet switching is a method of transmitting data from one computer to another that serves as the fundamental framework of how the Internet works. This meant that ARPANET facilitated what is known as peer-to-peer networking. Where most computer networks in the 1960s were hierarchal, meaning that certain computers performed control functions and other computers had to wait for permission to transmit data from the controller computers, every computer connected to ARPANET had equal privileges. In addition, ARPANET was designed to be transparent to applications, meaning that new Internet applications could be created and implemented from end user devices without any changes having to be made to the network itself. These features made ARPANET an incredibly capable and versatile means of communication.

ARPANET remained a military-only entity until the 1980s, when part of the network was made available for civilian use. The civilian portion of ARPANET became known as NSFnet in recognition of the National Science Foundation's supportive involvement with the network. At this stage, access to NSFnet was restricted to educational institutions and nonprofit organizations. Some of the earliest supercomputing centers to connect to NSFnet included the San Diego Supercomputer Center at the University of California, San Diego; the National Center for Supercomputing Applications at the University of Illinois; and the John von Neumann center at Princeton University. As the possibilities of NSFnet became increasingly apparent, however, a growing desire to utilize the network for commercial purposes soon encouraged another monumental step forward.

In response to the growing demand for network access, NSFnet was commercialized in 1991, thus giving birth to the modern Internet. It was not until 1993, however, that the Internet truly began to take on the look and feel with which it is recognizable today. That year, English computer scientist Tim Berners-Lee invented a critical software innovation known as the World Wide Web. The World Wide Web was an information system composed of interlinked hypertext documents that could be accessed over the Internet. In truth, much of what society aesthetically thinks of as the Internet today is actually the World Wide Web. With the advent of this breakthrough development, the commercialized Internet exploded in popularity and quickly became a global phenomenon that revolutionized everything from basic communications to commerce, entertainment, politics, and more. Eventually, as the means of Internet connectivity were improved and Internet access gradually grew faster and more reliable, the Internet became an increasingly ingrained part of everyday life. Today, the Internet is effectively everywhere all the time, a virtually inescapable entity that has evolved into an inexorable part of modern life.

Opposing Viewpoints: The Internet examines the status of Internet access as a human right and other issues surrounding this modern innovation in chapters titled "How Should the Internet Be Governed?," "How Does the Internet Impact the World?," "What Challenges Does the Internet Pose?," and "Can the Internet Be Dangerous?" As the Internet becomes a bigger part of daily life, society is faced with an ever growing barrage of questions about its governance and freedom of use, how it affects the world, and more. This volume offers insight into these topics from an array of different perspectives.

 **OPPOSING VIEWPOINTS® SERIES**

How Should the Internet Be Governed?

Chapter Preface

As the Internet has come to play a larger part in modern life, its ever expanding use has led to numerous practical, political, and social challenges that still need to be addressed. One of these challenges is the issue of Internet governance. The questions of who should control the Internet, how it should be controlled, and what rules for its use should be enforced loom large over the future of the online world. Since the Internet is a global communications tool, these questions must be addressed on a global scale. As such, Internet governance is a politically charged topic that will undoubtedly require a great deal of cooperation and compromise to properly address.

Not all issues related to Internet governance are global, however. Within the United States, government officials and communications corporations continue to debate how the Internet should be governed and operated on a national level. One of the major concerns in this domestic debate over the Internet is the issue of net neutrality. Since its earliest stages, the Internet has operated on a framework of net neutrality, which is the principle that all Internet users should have open, unrestricted access to all online content without any sort of purposeful blocking, deliberate traffic discrimination, or intentional slowdowns. Simply put, net neutrality is the foundation of the open Internet.

Over the years, net neutrality has been a sticking point between Internet service providers (ISPs) and the Federal Communications Commission (FCC), the federal government organization responsible for regulating the Internet. To maximize efficiency and minimize delays, ISPs have developed and employed specialized management techniques that prioritize certain types of Internet traffic. While this approach can be effective, critics contend that such prioritization is a threat to the future of net neutrality, particularly if ISPs are allowed to offer priority at cost for users willing and able to pay a fee for the fastest possible Internet service. This, in turn, would enable ISPs to work hand in hand with online content providers to create a tiered system of Internet access. Critics also worry that without net neutrality, ISPs could potentially use their control over the Internet to suppress competition in the online marketplace.

In 2010, in an effort to ensure the continuation of net neutrality, the FCC issued three important net neutrality rules: the transparency rule, the no blocking rule, and the no unreasonable discrimination rule. The transparency rule stated that ISPs have an obligation to be more open about their activities by disclosing intentional network slowdowns or usage caps to their customers. The no blocking rule stated that ISPs are not allowed to block applications or services at will simply to improve network performance. Finally, the no unreasonable discrimination rule stated that ISPs cannot discriminate against specific applications.

Since the FCC's 2010 net neutrality rules took effect, ISPs have been challenging the agency's authority. Resistance to net neutrality came to a head in 2014, when FCC chairman Tom Wheeler introduced a new plan that was set to end net neutrality and give ISPs the right to create pay-to-play fast lanes. However, opponents of this plan rallied against the proposed changes, ultimately forcing Wheeler to relent. In 2015 the FCC subsequently developed and enacted new net neutrality rules that offered Internet users stronger protections than ever before. While it is still a hotly debated issue, it looks as though net neutrality will remain the guiding principle of Internet use in America for the foreseeable future.

The following chapter explores net neutrality and other issues surrounding how the Internet should be governed.

> *"The world requires new rules that will empower and enable more and more people to tap into the full promise of human existence, while not simultaneously undercutting and diminishing that promise."*

Is Unrestricted Internet Access a Modern Human Right?

David Rothkopf

In the following viewpoint, David Rothkopf argues that Internet access should be considered a basic human right. Specifically, he contends that the Internet should be treated as a fundamental right because access to cyberspace has become a virtual necessity for communicating in the modern world. For that reason, he believes that everyone should have the opportunity to connect to the Internet. Rothkopf is the chief executive officer and editor of the Foreign Policy Group as well as the author of several books, including National Insecurity: American Leadership in an Age of Fear.

As you read, consider the following questions:

1. According to Rothkopf, how is Internet access similar to the press or firearms in terms of the US Constitution?

2. According to Rothkopf, why is Internet access likely to become an increasingly valuable commodity in the years to come?

3. According to the viewpoint, what impact would the classification of Internet access as a human right potentially have on the need for energy resources?

National constitutions are supposed to enshrine fundamental rights for everyone—and for generations. Such documents are also products of moments in time and reflect perceptions of life in those moments. That's why the best of them, like the U.S. Constitution, contain the seeds of their own reinvention. Indeed, the secret to a sustainable constitution is that it both captures what is enduring and anticipates the need to change.

Over the years, the U.S. Constitution has been amended 27 times—the first 10 being the Bill of Rights, of course—to ensure that it stays current with prevailing views of what is fundamental or best for the United States. Among the finest examples of the Constitution's adaptability to shifting and maturing norms are the 13th Amendment, which ended slavery, and the 15th and 19th Amendments, which guaranteed voting rights for everyone, regardless of race or gender, respectively.

Because it is meant to be malleable, the original Constitution included references to very few technologies. In fact, America's founders were so sure that technologies would evolve over time that they even included protection of the rights of innovators in Article 1, Section 8 (the copyright clause). The technologies that were mentioned were ones that by the late 1700s had become so ingrained in day-to-day life that they were seen as natural to the course of human existence, or at least critical to the functioning of government: money, for instance, and a military. In at least two cases in the Bill of Rights, the unfettered use of technologies was seen as necessary for citizens' freedom—those technologies being the press and arms. The press was more than three centuries old when the Constitution enshrined the right to freedom of expression. Meanwhile, the arms referenced were not specified, but no doubt included the firearms of the day that were essential to the upkeep of a militia, which was the express rationale (even if today it is generally overlooked) for the right to bear arms in the first place.

To be sure, technological progress challenges the assumptions that underlie even the best-conceived documents. This has been evident recently in the debate over whether Fourth Amendment guarantees against illegal searches and seizures, which explicitly pertain to the main information technology of the late 1700s ("papers"), cover technologies that have developed subsequently, such as e-mail and metadata. And, surprisingly, there has not been more meaningful debate about whether the Constitution protects the use of arms that Madison & Co. could not possibly have foreseen—namely, modern assault weapons—and how the Second Amendment applies in a world without militias.

Arguing that people cannot assert rights beyond the imagination of the Constitution's framers is an absurdity, and a dangerous one. As the metadata instance shows, it is hazardous not to bring the American conception of rights in line with the ways and means of modern life. Just as it took the invention of the printing press to trigger a deliberation on freedom of expression, technological changes today are so profound that they demand a reconsideration of what constitutes a fundamental right.

In recent years, more people have maintained that the right to unfettered Internet access is the modern equivalent of the right to the comparable technologies of centuries ago. The U.N. special rapporteur on freedom of opinion and expression has argued that disconnecting people from the Internet constitutes a human rights violation. A number of countries, in-

Access to the Internet and the Necessary Infrastructure

Given that the Internet has become an indispensable tool for realizing a range of human rights, combating inequality, and accelerating development and human progress, ensuring universal access to the Internet should be a priority for all states. Each state should thus develop a concrete and effective policy, in consultation with individuals from all sections of society, including the private sector and relevant government ministries, to make the Internet widely available, accessible and affordable to all segments of population.

Frank La Rue, "Report of the Special Rapporteur on the Promotion and Protection of the Right to Freedom of Opinion and Expression," United Nations General Assembly, May 16, 2011.

cluding Costa Rica, Estonia, Finland, France, Greece, and Spain, have asserted some right of access in their constitutions or legal codes, or via judicial rulings. Meanwhile, some advocates, such as Internet co-inventor Vint Cerf, have argued that content on the Internet must be protected from censorship, lest people's right to information be lost.

The thrust of these arguments converges on a single point: It is difficult, if not impossible in some places, to participate fully in today's world without an open, available Internet. This will become even truer as access is increasingly required to win and perform jobs, gather news, participate in politics, receive education, connect with health-care systems, and engage in basic financial services. (Coin and paper money, one of those few technologies mentioned in the U.S. Constitution, will fade in importance in coming decades, outmoded by mobile banking.)

These are daunting thoughts on a planet on which 4.4 billion people lack Internet access—but that number is shrinking rapidly. The International Telecommunication Union projected in May 2014 that 3 billion people would be online by the end of 2014, up some 300 million from the previous year's projection. In a July 2014 report, based on a canvass of more than 1,400 experts, the Pew Research Center found that even though governments will likely find new ways to restrict Internet access and content, billions more people may be online by 2025. Microsoft has estimated that number will be close to 5 billion.

This revolution carries with it other important questions. If there is a right to the Internet, for instance, does that mean people must also have a right to the electricity needed to plug into the web? The answer, resoundingly, is yes—even though, in a great tragedy of multilateralism, the creators of the Millennium Development Goals failed to set a benchmark for energy access. Electricity once seemed a luxury, but today the nearly 1.3 billion without it are effectively cut off from modern life. Yet this raises another question: In a world where roughly 80 percent of electricity is—and for a long time will be—produced by burning fossil fuels, how is the right to a clean, healthy environment also protected? This points to a need for universal access to clean, sustainable, and affordable energy.

Abstract as a discussion of fundamental rights may seem, determining what people must have to survive and thrive, and wrestling with the conflicts found among these elements, may represent the greatest challenge of this century. The world requires new rules that will empower and enable more and more people to tap into the full promise of human existence, while not simultaneously undercutting and diminishing that promise.

These rules are being made possible by technological advances, but they will not actually come to be if leaders do not act to create them—if governments leave it to the happenstance of progress to sort out tensions among the modern ingredients of life, liberty, and the pursuit of happiness. The conversation about necessary action is already coming too late. The longer it takes to kick into high gear, the longer humans will continue hurtling toward a new economic and social reality. Simultaneously, there will be much slower progress toward ensuring that the gains this reality brings are not offset by the tragedy of too few people benefiting or by the planet's gradual but irreversible degradation.

"Rights based on human freedoms are the only human rights. Any other characterisation misses the fact that human rights are those that must be able to exist in absence of the state."

Internet Access Should Not Be Treated as a Human Right

Simon Breheny

In the following viewpoint, Simon Breheny argues that access to the Internet should not be treated as a basic human right. In making his point, Breheny alleges that the interpretation of Internet access as a human right is a fallacy that has arisen from liberals' tendency to skew the true definition of human rights for political gain. Breheny is an Australian author and the director of the Legal Rights Project at the Institute of Public Affairs in Melbourne, Australia.

As you read, consider the following questions:

1. According Breheny, why are things such as health care and education not truly human rights?

2. According to Breheny, why has the left-wing co-opted human rights, and what effect has that phenomenon had?

Simon Breheny, "How the Left Corrupted Human Rights," *IPA Review*, November 2013. Copyright © 2013 IPA Review. Reproduced by permission.

3. According to Breheny, what constitutes a true human right?

In May 2011, a United Nations [UN] special rapporteur declared that people had a human right to Internet access. It seems absurd to argue that such a right exists but it is the logical progression of the corrupting influence of leftist ideology on the traditional conception of human rights.

It's worth pointing out that this is not just an obscure debate within the confines of an irrelevant international body. Finland had implemented legislation a year before—in July 2010—that granted every one of its citizens the right to speeds of one megabit per second.

The right to Internet access is just one of the many 'human rights' manufactured by the left throughout the course of the last century. The right to welfare is another example. Earlier this year [2013], another UN official said that an Australian government decision to reduce welfare payments was a violation of the unemployed's fundamental right to receive Centrelink [governmental payments and services to those in need] benefits.

The Left and Rights Throughout History

'Rights' to other social privileges have also become popular over the last hundred years. During his State of the Union address on 11 January 1944, US president Franklin D. Roosevelt proposed a 'Second Bill of Rights.' This new Bill of Rights included rights to employment, a living wage, freedom from unfair competition and monopolies, housing, medical care, education and social security. FDR believed that the US's original Bill of Rights had 'proved inadequate to assure us equality in the pursuit of happiness.'

A similar set of 'human rights' was later included in the 1952 Universal Declaration of Human Rights. The Universal Declaration included rights to employment (article 23), housing, health care and welfare (article 25) and education (article 26). If the Internet had been around in the 1950s, the right to bandwidth probably would have been included, too.

Of course, none of these things are actually human rights. At best they're vague policy aspirations. By definition, human rights exist without the need for policies and programs of government. Universal human rights are not privileges granted by the state but restrictions on what the state can do. The concept of human rights is based on the idea that people acquire them by virtue of being human. So if coercion is required to give effect to a potential human right, it's not a human right. Compulsory redistribution of resources of the kind that is required for government programs such as subsidised education and health care are therefore not human rights.

The Problem with False Rights

The fundamental issue with this group of so-called rights is not just that they don't meet the definition of human rights. That would be a pretty abstract concern. The deeper concern is that their implementation unavoidably entails their violation.

Rights to free schooling, housing, jobs, and health care require the government to take money from one section of the community and give it to another.

This is just old-fashioned redistribution and it clearly violates your human right to do with your property what you will. But it's sold under the guise of human rights.

And a strikingly large number of people accept that these are in fact rights to which we as human beings are entitled. It is remarkable that so many have come to accept these vague policy goals as immutable rights. And it's important to understand why.

The key reason these 'rights' were developed was to achieve particular ideological ends. While conservatives and liberals see human rights as an end in themselves, the left-wing views human rights as another tool to achieve outcomes. And it's for this reason that leftists have co-opted the language of human rights. It's not hard to see why. What's more powerful: 'I think the government should subsidise education,' or 'people have a right to free education.'

Rights in Politics

The language of human rights has been used very successfully by the left to fight for particular interest groups they have decided are important. It allows the left to elevate left-wing principles of equality to the same level as human liberty.

The left's co-optation of the language of traditional human rights to their own agenda has corrupted human rights. Original ideas about civil liberties place a distant second in the minds of many human rights lawyers and academics, if they even figure at all.

More particularly, the left has corrupted legitimate human rights that broadly fall into the category of 'positive liberties.' In his 1958 essay 'Two Concepts of Liberty,' Isaiah Berlin argued that there are two categories of freedom—positive and negative liberties. Negative liberties are those that exist when an individual is free from coercion. Freedom of thought and association, for example, are respected simply by the state doing nothing to restrict these rights. Rights to participate in the political system are distinct—they require some level of government action. The right to vote is a positive liberty.

The success of the left was in twisting Berlinian positive liberties into what they now call positive rights. This co-optation by progressives was successfully used to include what became known as economic, social and cultural rights. The International Covenant on Economic, Social and Cultural Rights is the best example of this. The UN treaty is filled with the kind of vague 'rights' loved by those on the left. Of course, due to their ambiguity it is impossible to objectively enforce these rights because they require qualitative measurements.

In stark contrast, the International Covenant on Civil and Political Rights defends true human rights. Civil rights are negative freedoms, while political rights are positive freedoms in the classical sense.

The True Nature of Rights

True human rights are rooted in the idea that individuals should be free to pursue their own goals. They go to the heart of classical liberal philosophy—human rights act as specific limits on state power and create the blueprint for legitimate government built on the protection of human rights, not their abrogation.

Rights based on human freedoms are the only human rights. Any other characterisation misses the fact that human rights are those that must be able to exist in absence of the state. The left has clearly failed to grasp this important idea. But conservatives and liberals have also failed to address this corruption. It's time for us to take on the left and return to a truly liberal conception of human rights.

*"The Obama administration should fo-
cus its energy and resources on net neutrality and make sure that the FCC
does the right thing for the U.S. and
global economies."*

Net Neutrality Is an Important Principle

Marvin Ammori

*In the following viewpoint, Marvin Ammori argues that the
principle of net neutrality is a necessity that must be maintained
if the Internet is to remain open and free. Offering detailed information on the political debate over net neutrality, Ammori
contends that Washington must unequivocally support net neutrality or risk turning the Internet into a fragmented series of
fiefdoms that will ultimately be detrimental to the freedom of
information and the health of the American economy. Ammori is
a lawyer and activist who specializes in the area of Internet freedom.*

As you read, consider the following questions:

1. According to Ammori, why should the FCC have more
   control over ISPs?

Marvin Ammori, "The Case for Net Neutrality: What's Wrong with Obama's Internet
Policy," *Foreign Affairs*, July–August 2014. Copyright © 2014 Foreign Affairs. Reproduced
by permission.

2. According to the viewpoint, what effect would the end of net neutrality likely have on American entrepreneurs' business interests in foreign markets?

3. According to Ammori, what needs to be done to ensure the survival of net neutrality?

For all the withering criticism leveled at the White House for its botched rollout of HealthCare.gov, that debacle is not the biggest technology-related failure of Barack Obama's presidency. That inauspicious distinction belongs to his administration's incompetence in another area: reneging on Obama's signature pledge to ensure "net neutrality," the straightforward but powerful idea that Internet service providers (ISPs) should treat all traffic that goes through their networks the same. Net neutrality holds that ISPs shouldn't offer preferential treatment to some websites over others or charge some companies arbitrary fees to reach users. By this logic, AT&T, for example, shouldn't be allowed to grant iTunes Radio a special "fast lane" for its data while forcing Spotify to make do with choppier service.

On the campaign trail in 2007, Obama called himself "a strong supporter of net neutrality" and promised that under his administration, the Federal Communications Commission [FCC] would defend that principle. But in the last few months, his FCC appears to have given up on the goal of maintaining an open Internet. This past January [in 2014], a U.S. federal appeals court, in a case brought by Verizon, struck down the net neutrality rules adopted by the FCC in 2010, which came close to fulfilling Obama's pledge despite a few loopholes. Shortly after the court's decision, Netflix was reportedly forced to pay Comcast tens of millions of dollars per year to ensure that Netflix users who connect to the Internet through Comcast could stream movies reliably; Apple reportedly entered into its own negotiations with Comcast to secure its own special treatment. Sensing an opening, AT&T and Verizon filed legal documents urging the FCC to allow them to set up a new pricing scheme in which they could charge every website a different price for such special treatment.

Obama wasn't responsible for the court's decision, but in late April, the administration signaled that it would reverse course on net neutrality and give ISPs just what they wanted. FCC chair Tom Wheeler circulated a proposal to the FCC's four other commissioners, two Democrats and two Republicans, for rules that would allow broadband providers to charge content providers for faster, smoother service. The proposal would also authorize ISPs to make exclusive deals with particular providers, so that PayPal could be the official payment processor for Verizon, for example, or Amazon Prime could be the official video provider for Time Warner Cable.

Word of the proposal leaked to the press and sparked an immediate backlash. One hundred and fifty leading technology companies, including Amazon, Microsoft, and Kickstarter, sent a letter to the FCC calling the plan a "grave threat to the Internet." In their own letter to the FCC, over 100 of the nation's leading venture capital investors wrote that the proposal, if adopted as law, would "stifle innovation," since many start-ups and entrepreneurs wouldn't be able to afford to access a fast lane. Activist groups organized protests outside the FCC's headquarters in Washington and accused Wheeler, a former lobbyist for both the cable and the wireless industries, of favoring his old clients over the public interest. Nonetheless, on May 15, the FCC released its official proposal, concluding tentatively that it could authorize fast lanes and slow lanes on the Internet. Although the FCC is now officially gathering feedback on that proposal, it has promised to adopt a final rule by the end of this year.

The FCC and ISPs

Despite the missteps so far, the administration still has a second chance to fix its Internet policy, just as it did with Health

Care.gov. Preferably working with policy makers of all stripes supportive of open markets, it should ensure that the FCC adopts rules that maintain the Internet as basic infrastructure that can be used by entrepreneurs, businesses, and average citizens alike—not a limited service controlled by a few large corporations. In the arcane world of federal administrative agencies, that guarantee comes down to whether the FCC adopts rules that rely on flimsy legal grounds, as it has in the past, or ones that rely on the solid foundation of its main regulatory authority over "common carriers," the legal term the U.S. government uses to describe firms that transport people, goods, or messages for a fee, such as trains and telephone companies. In 1910, Congress designated telephone wires as a common carrier service and decreed that the federal government should regulate electronic information traveling over wires in the same way that it regulated the movement of goods and passengers on railroads across state lines through the now defunct Interstate Commerce Commission, which meant that Congress could prevent companies from engaging in discrimination and charging unreasonable access fees. When the FCC was created in 1934 by the Communications Act, those common carrier rules were entrusted to it through a section of the law known as Title II. Today, the broadband wires and networks on which the Internet relies are the modern-day equivalent of these phone lines, and they should be regulated as such: Like telephone companies before them, ISPs should be considered common carriers. This classification is crucial to protecting the Internet as public infrastructure that users can access equally, whether they run a multinational corporation or write a political blog.

However, in 2002, Michael Powell, then chair of the FCC, classified ISPs not as common carriers but as "an information service," which has handicapped the FCC's ability to enforce net neutrality and regulate ISPs ever since. If ISPs are not reclassified as common carriers, Internet infrastructure will suffer. By authorizing payments for fast lanes, the FCC will encourage ISPs to cater to those customers able and willing to pay a premium, at the expense of upgrading infrastructure for those in the slow lanes.

The stakes for the U.S. economy are high: Failing to ban ISPs from discriminating against companies would make it harder for tech entrepreneurs to compete, because the costs of entry would rise and ISPs could seek to hobble service for competitors unwilling or unable to pay special access fees. Foreign countries would likely follow Washington's lead, enacting protectionist measures that would close off foreign markets to U.S. companies. But the harm would extend even further. Given how much the Internet has woven itself into every aspect of daily life, the laws governing it shape economic and political decisions around the world and affect every industry, almost every business, and billions of people. If the Obama administration fails to reverse course on net neutrality, the Internet could turn into a patchwork of fiefdoms, with untold ripple effects.

Innovation Superhighway

Net neutrality is not some esoteric concern; it has been a major contributor to the success of the Internet economy. Unlike in the late 1990s, when users accessed relatively hived-off areas of cyberspace through slow dial-up connections, the Internet is now defined by integration. The credit for this improvement goes to high-speed connections, cellular networks, and short-distance wireless technologies such as Wi-Fi and Bluetooth, which have allowed companies large and small—from Google to Etsy—to link up computers, smartphones, tablets, and wearable electronics. But all this integration has relied on a critical feature of the global Internet: No one needs permission from anyone to do anything.

Historically, ISPs have acted as gateways to all the wonderful (or not so wonderful) things connected to the Internet.

But they have not acted as gatekeepers, determining which files and servers should load better or worse. From day one, the Internet was a public square, and the providers merely connected everyone, rather than regulating who spoke with whom. That allowed the Internet to evolve into a form of basic infrastructure, used by over a billion people today.

The Internet's openness has radically transformed all kinds of industries, from food delivery to finance, by lowering the barriers to entry. It has allowed a few bright engineers or students with an idea to launch a business that would be immediately available all over the world to over a billion potential customers. Start-ups don't need the leverage and bank accounts of Apple or Google to get reliable service to reach their users. In fact, historically, they have not paid any arbitrary fees to providers to reach users. Their costs often involve nothing more than hard work, inexpensive cloud computing tools, and off-the-shelf laptops and mobile devices, which are getting more powerful and cheaper by the day. As Marc Andreessen, a cofounder of Netscape and a venture capitalist, has pointed out, the cost of running a basic Internet application fell from $150,000 a month in 2000 to $1,500 a month in 2011. It continues to fall.

In some ways, the Internet is just the latest and perhaps most impressive of what economists call "general-purpose technologies," from the steam engine to the electricity grid, all of which, since their inception, have had a massively disproportionate impact on innovation and economic growth. In a 2012 report, the Boston Consulting Group found that the Internet economy accounted for 4.1 percent (about $2.3 trillion) of GDP [gross domestic product] in the G20 countries [a group whose membership includes a mix of the world's largest advanced and emerging economies] in 2010. If the Internet were a national economy, the report noted, it would be among the five largest in the world, ahead of Germany. And a 2013 [Ewing Marion] Kauffman Foundation report showed that in the previous three decades, the high-tech sector was 23 percent more likely, and the information technology sector 48 percent more likely, to give birth to new businesses than the private sector overall.

That growth, impressive as it is, could be just the beginning, as everyday objects, such as household devices and cars, go online as part of "the Internet of Things." John Chambers, the CEO [chief executive officer] of Cisco Systems, has predicted that the Internet of Things could create a $19 trillion market in the near future. Mobile-based markets will only expand, too; the Boston Consulting Group projects that mobile devices will account for four out of five broadband connections by 2016.

Not Neutrality

All this innovation has taken place without the permission of ISPs. But that could change as net neutrality comes under threat. ISPs have consistently maintained that net neutrality is a solution in search of a problem, but this often-repeated phrase is simply wrong. In the United States, both small and large providers have already violated the very principles that net neutrality is designed to protect. Ever since 2005, the FCC has pursued a policy that resembles net neutrality but that allows enough room for interpretation for firms to find ways to undermine it. From 2005 to 2008, the largest ISP in the United States, Comcast, used technologies that monitor all the data coming from users to secretly block so-called peer-to-peer technologies, such as BitTorrent and Gnutella. These tools are popular for streaming online TV (sometimes illegally), using cloud-based storage and sharing services such as those provided by Amazon, and communicating through online phone services such as Skype. In 2005, a small ISP in North Carolina called Madison River Communications blocked Vonage, a company that allows customers to make cheap domestic and international telephone calls over the Internet. From 2007 to

2009, AT&T's contract with Apple required the latter to block Skype and other competing phone services on the iPhone, so that customers could not use them when connected to a cellular network. From 2011 to 2013, AT&T, Sprint, and Verizon blocked all the functionality of Google Wallet, a mobile payment system, on Google Nexus smartphones, likely because all three providers are part of a competing joint venture called Isis.

In the EU [European Union], widespread violations of net neutrality affect at least one in five users, according to a 2012 report from the Body of European Regulators for Electronic Communications. Restrictions affect everything from online phone services and peer-to-peer technologies to gaming applications and e-mail. In 2011, the Netherlands' dominant mobile carrier, KPN, saw that its text messaging revenue was plummeting and made moves to block applications such as WhatsApp and Skype, which allow users to send free texts. Across the Atlantic, in 2005, the Canadian telecommunications company Telus used its control of the wires to block the website of a union member taking part in a strike against the company.

Opponents of net neutrality insist that efforts to enforce it are unnecessary, because market competition will ensure that companies act in their customers' best interests. But true competition doesn't exist among ISPs. In the United States, local cable monopolies are often the only game in town when it comes to high-speed access and usually control over two-thirds of the market. In places where there are real options, users rarely switch services because of the penalties that providers charge them for terminating their contracts early.

Some skeptics of strong regulation have proposed rules requiring companies merely to disclose their technical discrimination policies, but those wouldn't solve the problem either. Even in the United Kingdom, which boasts both healthy competition among ISPs and robust disclosure laws, companies still frequently discriminate against various types of Internet traffic. Indeed, wherever you look, the absence of rules enforcing net neutrality virtually guarantees that someone will violate the principle. As it stands now, after the FCC's rules were struck down in January, U.S. law does little to protect net neutrality. As companies push the boundaries, violations will become more common—and not just in the United States.

If the FCC doesn't rein in U.S. ISPs, there is likely to be a domino effect abroad. Some foreign officials view the net neutrality movement as nothing more than an attempt to protect U.S. technology companies, since given their size, they are the main beneficiaries of net neutrality abroad. (Twitter, for example, does well in foreign markets only where the government doesn't block it and carriers don't charge extra for it.) Foreign ISPs have long hoped to exclude U.S. companies from their markets or at least charge them for access, and if U.S. providers are allowed to play similar games in the United States, it will give foreign governments the perfect excuse to give their ISPs what they want. Similarly, if the U.S. government continues to allow American ISPs to block or charge foreign technology companies, such as Spotify, which is based in Sweden, then sooner or later, other countries are likely to retaliate by giving their own providers a similar right. The result would be a global patchwork of fees and discriminatory rules.

Another danger is that if the Internet becomes less open in the United States, some forward-thinking foreign governments could enhance their net neutrality protections as a way of luring U.S. entrepreneurs and engineers to move abroad. Soon after the U.S. federal appeals court struck down the FCC's net neutrality rules in January, Neelie Kroes, a vice president of the European Commission who is responsible for its digital agenda, asked on Twitter if she should "invite newly disadvantaged US start-ups to [the] EU, so they have a fair chance." By early April, the European Parliament had adopted

© David Fitzsimmons, "Net Neutrality," Cagle Post, November 17, 2013.

tough net neutrality rules. Likewise, Chile, the first nation to adopt net neutrality rules, in 2010, has sought to attract global entrepreneurs through a government initiative called Start-Up Chile, which has invested millions of dollars in hundreds of foreign technology companies, most of which hail from the United States.

Life in the Slow Lane

Imagine if, years ago, Myspace had cut deals with cable and phone companies to block Facebook, if Lycos had colluded with AltaVista to crush Google, if Microsoft had contracted with service providers to protect Internet Explorer by blocking Mozilla Firefox. If ISPs are allowed to block, discriminate, and charge for different applications, such scenarios could become commonplace. The main reason they have not been is because the FCC, in 2005, stated that Internet access should be "operated in a neutral manner" and subsequently stepped in a few times to enforce that policy: against Madison River Communications regarding Vonage, against Comcast regarding peer-to-peer services, and against AT&T and Apple regarding Skype. The enforcement has not been completely consistent—in store payments from Google Wallet are still being blocked on AT&T's, Verizon's, and T-Mobile's wireless networks—but it has still largely succeeded in imposing some discipline on the market.

Without that FCC regulation, the Internet would have come to look very different than it does today—a lot more like the cable industry, in fact. For decades, cable companies, such as Comcast and Time Warner Cable, and satellite TV providers, such as DirecTV, have acquired equity stakes in channels as part of their carriage deals. That arrangement has resulted in disputes over price tiers, with smaller channels claiming they get put into more expensive, limited service packages than a cable company's own channels. In a lengthy dispute with Comcast, for example, the independently owned Tennis Channel argued that it should be placed in the same basic service package as the Golf Channel and the NBC Sports Network, two sports channels that Comcast owns and provides to all its subscribers. In May 2013, a U.S. federal appeals court ruled in Comcast's favor; the Tennis Channel appealed to the Supreme Court, which in February declined to hear the case. Internet companies have never had to give up equity stakes as part of service deals to reach users or had to compete with firms that are owned by ISPs and thus given preferential treatment. And most of them would have run out of funding during the years of litigation if they had taken legal action like the Tennis Channel has.

A scenario in which websites have to acquiesce to ISPs in order to secure competitive access to the Internet would kill innovation. Small companies would no longer be able to reach every segment of the market at no extra cost. A new company's rivals, if they could afford it, would be able to pay for better service, thereby reducing consumers' choices. Many start-ups would be unable to pay expensive access fees and would simply not start up in the first place. Investors would end up putting larger sums in fewer companies, and with no clear limit on how much ISPs could charge, the potential rewards from successful investments might be smaller and would certainly be more uncertain than they are today.

It is unrealistic to expect competition among ISPs to prevent or limit such fees; it hasn't done so in the United Kingdom and other European markets. Nor can one argue that ISPs need the money. They already enjoy comically high profit margins on broadband delivery, and their operating costs continue to decrease. In weighing the potential damage to entrepreneurship against the financial gains of a few huge telecommunications companies, the U.S. government should back the entrepreneurs.

That's especially so since without net neutrality, telecommunications and cable companies could also stifle free expression by favoring the websites and applications of the largest media conglomerates over those of nonprofit news organizations, bloggers, and independent journalists and filmmakers. Permitting media giants to pay for a fast lane unavailable to all online outlets would raise the barriers to entry for all new publishing and sharing tools—eliminating innovations along the lines of Twitter, Tumblr, and WordPress. These tools, most of which started with extremely small investments, have helped citizens find new ways to petition and protest against their governments. New and better tools of this kind will continue to emerge only if the field is left open.

Keeping the Internet Open

The Obama administration needs to get the rules governing the Internet right. Obama's initial, feeble attempts to do so came during his first term, when the FCC was chaired by Julius Genachowski, a law school classmate of Obama's who demonstrated a distinct lack of political insight and courage on the job. In 2010, the FCC adopted a set of net neutrality rules known as the Open Internet Order, which barred providers from blocking or giving preferential access to particular websites and applications and required more disclosure about their policies. Moreover, in the order, the FCC effectively prohibited ISPs from creating and charging for fast lanes, declaring them unreasonable. But under pressure from ISPs, Genachowski punched two gaping loopholes into these rules. He exempted mobile access from the order, even though more people now go online through their cell phones than through their home computers. He also made it possible for ISPs to violate net neutrality through connection deals that they make directly with websites—a loophole that Comcast has exploited in its shakedown of Netflix.

Ultimately, however, it was the FCC's 2002 definition of ISPs as "an information service," rather than a "common carrier," that overwhelmed the weak rules established in 2010. Last year, Verizon challenged the 2010 rules, arguing that they went beyond the FCC's jurisdiction given the commission's own classification of ISPs as an information service. Since they were not common carriers, they could not be regulated according to Title II of the Communications Act, which would allow the FCC to treat them like telephone companies and ban unreasonable Internet discrimination and access fees. In January, a U.S. federal appeals court agreed with Verizon and struck down the 2010 FCC rules.

In legal terms, the FCC can easily address all these issues when it adopts a new order later this year. By reclassifying ISPs as common carriers, the FCC could regulate them as it does phone companies. It should not shy away from using the authority that Congress gave it; the Supreme Court, in 2005, made clear that the FCC has the power to change ISPs' classification. Getting the legal definition right is crucial, since the FCC's last two attempts to enforce net neutrality were struck down in court on jurisdictional grounds, first in April 2010, in a case brought by Comcast, and then in January of this year. In both cases, rather than relying on its main authority over common carriers under Title II, the FCC attempted to impose net neutrality requirements through weaker regulatory authorities, including Section 706 of the Telecommunications Act of 1996, which gives the FCC the authority to regulate broadband infrastructure deployment. Each time, the court's ruling was sharply dismissive of the FCC's legal reasoning, as nondiscrimination rules can be applied only to common carriers.

In addition to fixing the FCC's legal footing, the new order should close the two loopholes in the moribund 2010 rules. First, there should be no exceptions for restrictions on mobile access. That is particularly important since many start-ups now develop applications initially or even exclusively for mobile phones, such as Instagram and Uber. The FCC should also make clear that ISPs cannot charge websites for direct connections to their networks, as Comcast has done with Netflix.

But Wheeler, Obama's FCC chair, has indicated that he prefers a different path. In late April, in an attempt at damage control after the FCC's new proposed rules were leaked, Wheeler wrote in a blog post on the FCC's website that he wouldn't "hesitate to use Title II" at some undefined future date. But instead of invoking those powers directly, the May 15 proposal tentatively concluded that the FCC would again rely on Section 706 of the Telecommunications Act as the basis for its legal authority, although it did say that it would also consider the use of Title II. Section 706 is the same flawed authority that the FCC already relied on in its 2010 rules and that the appeals court in January already held could not support restrictions against discrimination or fast lanes. Wheeler appears to have chosen this path because it is easier politically; the ISPs will not complain, since they are getting everything they wanted.

Although the Obama administration and the FCC are the main decision makers, Republicans should recognize the need to support an open Internet. Over the years, some Republicans, including former FCC chair Kevin Martin, who served under President George W. Bush; former House pepresentative Charles "Chip" Pickering; and former senator Olympia Snowe, have supported net neutrality as the best way to promote entrepreneurship, free-market competition, and free speech. Opposing an open Internet now would put the party on the wrong side of its values and on the wrong side of history.

A country's Internet infrastructure, just like its physical infrastructure, is essential to its economic competition and growth. According to the Organisation for Economic Cooperation and Development, high-speed Internet is not only slower in New York City and San Francisco than it is in Seoul; it also costs five times as much. Suffering from an even more expensive, less robust, and more fragmented Internet infrastructure would put the entire U.S. economy in a global slow lane.

Washington faces a simple choice: allow the Internet to remain an engine of innovation, a platform for speech in even the harshest tyrannies, and a unified connection for people across the globe—or cede control of the Internet to service providers motivated by their parochial interests. The Obama administration should focus its energy and resources on net neutrality and make sure that the FCC does the right thing for the U.S. and global economies. If it does not, many online businesses will soon have the kinds of problems usually associated with certain failed government websites.

VIEWPOINT 4

> "*Rather than guarding against market abuses by dominant firms, the rules have been invoked in attempts to hinder innovation, impede competition, and block consumer price protections.*"

Net Neutrality Is More Harmful than Helpful

James L. Gattuso

In the following viewpoint, James L. Gattuso argues against the enforcement of net neutrality rules. Citing the potential benefits for consumers of an unregulated Internet marketplace, Gattuso says that concerns over the end of net neutrality are greatly overstated and that fewer such rules will ultimately be better for everyone. Gattuso is a senior research fellow for regulatory policy with the Heritage Foundation's Thomas A. Roe Institute for Economic Policy Studies.

As you read, consider the following questions:

1. According to Gattuso, why was the FCC's 2005 decision about the nature of broadband Internet service the correct decision?

James L. Gattuso, "Net Neutrality Rules: Still a Threat to Internet Freedom," Heritage.org, February 12, 2014. © 2014 Heritage Foundation. Reproduced by permission.

2. According to Gattuso, why are net neutrality supporters' worries about an unregulated Internet unfounded?

3. Why is AT&T's sponsored data plan not a threat to Internet freedom, according to the viewpoint?

In a significant victory for American consumers, a federal appeals court struck down Federal Communications Commission (FCC) rules regulating broadband Internet service on January 14 [2014]. The much-anticipated decision clears the way for more investment, more innovation, and lower costs for Internet users. But the political battle over these "network neutrality" rules—which limit differentiation and prioritization of Internet traffic—is far from over. Legislation to reinstate FCC controls will almost certainly be considered in Congress. And, encouraged by supportive language in the circuit court opinion, the FCC may take another shot at the issue itself.

Web users should wish these efforts no success. Net neutrality rules were a dangerously bad idea when adopted by the FCC in 2010, and the experience of the past three years has only made the dangers clearer.

What Is Net Neutrality?

The term "network neutrality" refers to the principle that the owners of broadband networks (such as Verizon and Comcast) that serve end users should treat all communications travelling over their networks alike. The concept is based on longstanding practice but had never been enshrined in a governmental rule or regulation. In fact, in 2005, the FCC specifically declared that broadband Internet service was not a "telecommunications service," and thus not subject to common-carrier rules that bar variations in rates and services. Unlike traditional telephone companies and electric utilities, broadband providers would be free to establish their own business models in the marketplace.

This finding made sense. Broadband service was, and is, dynamic and growing, with the line between a successful investment and a failure a thin one. Differentiated offerings, such as discounts and priority-service plans are common in such markets. And, the market for broadband is a competitive one, with two or more major players in almost every service area, limiting the prospect for market abuse.

Nevertheless, at the same time that the FCC declared that broadband was not a "telecommunications service," it adopted a set of "guidelines" articulating neutrality principles. Although the FCC's principles were ostensibly nonbinding, in 2008, the agency ordered Comcast to stop alleged violations. That effort was put to a stop in early 2010 by a federal appeals court, which ruled that the FCC had not demonstrated that it had authority to regulate broadband communications.

In December 2010, the FCC returned to the issue, adopting formal rules limiting how Internet service providers (ISPs) could handle Internet traffic, and broadening its claim of authority. These net neutrality—or, as the FCC called them, "open Internet"—rules banned consumer wireline (DSL and cable modem) broadband providers from "unreasonably discriminat[ing] in transmitting lawful network traffic," and "block[ing] lawful content, applications, services, or 'non-harmful' devices."

Recognizing that wireless broadband service was especially dynamic and innovative, mobile service providers were subjected to slightly less burdensome rules. They were banned only from "block[ing] consumers from accessing lawful websites," and "applications that compete with the provider's voice or video telephony services."

Lastly, all providers were required to disclose their network management practices to the public.

The rules did not bar all forms of differentiation. Even the FCC recognized the limits of absolute neutrality. With increasing demands on the Internet, some steps to manage traffic (such as controlling bandwidth-hogging users) are critical. More generally, certain types of prioritization common in other industries—such as selling premium or discount access to certain web content providers—would also benefit users.

To address such beneficial differentiation, the FCC exempted "reasonable network management." But exactly what was "reasonable" was left undefined. The rules offered only vague and circular guidance, such as: "Reasonable network management shall not constitute unreasonable discrimination." This, of course, vested vast discretion in the five FCC members, who would determine case by case which ISP actions were acceptable and which ones were not. As a result, the FCC's ostensible softening of the rule by exempting "reasonable" management practices actually increased the agency's power once again.

The new rules were soon challenged in court by Verizon, claiming that the FCC lacked jurisdiction over broadband service. Last month's decision was the result of that litigation. As was the case in 2010, the FCC's rules were slapped down. Specifically, the court found that the regulations imposed on the ISPs were, in effect, common-carrier regulations. Since the FCC had previously ruled that the broadband service providers were not "telecommunication providers," the FCC was barred by law from imposing common-carrier regulations on them.

End of the Internet?

In the wake of the decision, there have been many dire but ill-founded predictions as to what the effects will be. Craig Aaron of the pro-regulation group Free Press argued that exclusive deals among providers "could become the norm, with AT&T exclusively bringing you Netflix, while Time Warner Cable is the sole source for YouTube." He sees privacy and choice heading toward the ash heap of history, saying, "it won't be long before your ISP requires you to connect via their list of approved devices and then uses those devices to literally watch you." To the question "Is this the end of the Internet?," he answers, "maybe."

Michael Weinberg of the advocacy group Public Knowledge similarly cites a parade of horribles, including degraded service, higher costs, and less innovation, due to higher fees and restricted choices.

Advocates of regulation, however, have been making such Chicken Little-esqe predictions for years, and they never seem to come true. ISPs are more interested in gaining users than driving them away. There has, in fact, been only one recorded case where an ISP clearly attempted to block Internet content for its own benefit. In the vast majority of cases, the imagined outrages of ISPs sabotaging rivals and extracting ruinous fees are just that, imagined.

Certainly, ISPs have the technical ability to block or impede certain services and websites. But they are hardly unique in that regard. Many firms, including Google—a longtime supporter of neutrality regulation—have similar abilities. Google, however, does not engage in inappropriate discrimination for the same reason that Verizon and Comcast do not: competition. Blocking websites or impeding disfavored services would quickly send customers packing to another provider.

A look at the actual disputes that have arisen under net neutrality over the past three years supports this conclusion. None of the instances where a violation of the rules was alleged involved a dominant provider abusing its market power. Nor did any involve additional fees; in fact, the most controversial practice involved a shift of fees *away* from consumers. On the other hand, the major controversies involved attempts to game the system, increase costs to consumers, and hinder competitive challenges. The disputes included:

Gaming the System: Comcast v. Level 3 [Communications] Fee. In November 2010, as the FCC was finalizing its now-void neutrality rules, a dispute broke out between Comcast and Internet "backbone" provider Level 3. As is common among such long-haul service providers, the two had long operated under a "peering" arrangement by which the two networks interconnected to allow them to transport traffic from its origin to its destination. Because the traffic load was about even in both directions, neither side paid a fee to the other.

This balance changed when Level 3 won a contract to carry content for Netflix, whose online video service was rapidly growing. At the time of the deal, Netflix accounted for 20 percent of all broadband traffic during peak hours. That meant that the amount of traffic that Level 3 sent to Comcast to deliver would balloon to five times the amount going the other way.

When Comcast asked to be paid for its additional interconnection service, pointing out that the traffic flows were now far from even, Level 3 balked. Comcast's fees, it argued, were a form of discrimination, unacceptable under neutrality principles. Neutrality restrictions, of course, were never meant to restrict firms in the highly competitive backbone Internet business, so Level 3—pointing to its Netflix business—simply redefined itself as a content provider for Netflix. Online petitions were soon circulating, asking the FCC to "Stop Comcast from blocking Netflix." Level 3 was expertly gaming the still-nascent rules. As Randolph May of the Free State Foundation put it at the time:

> Level 3, no stranger to Washington's regulatory playing fields, has converted what heretofore has been an ordinary commercial negotiation over the fees, if any, applicable to peering arrangements between two interconnecting Internet providers into a complaint sounding in—surprise!—net neutrality.

In the end, the two firms negotiated a compromise without FCC involvement. But the case shows how the blurry concept of neutrality can be gamed by players looking for a regulatory advantage in the marketplace.

No Lack of Competition: AT&T and FaceTime. In 2012, Apple upgraded its popular FaceTime application to enable consumers to use it over mobile phone networks. Previously consumers could only use it when accessing the Internet via Wi-Fi connections, and not through wireless telephone links. Despite Apple's move, AT&T continued to limit FaceTime usage on its own, only allowing subscribers of its "Mobile Share" unlimited data use plan to use it on the wireless telephone network. The restriction was necessary, AT&T argued, to protect its subscribers from congestion caused by a suddenly increased traffic load caused by the highly bandwidth-intensive FaceTime video service.

Critics immediately slammed the decision as illegal blocking of an application in violation of FCC neutrality rules. But if AT&T's aim was to stifle FaceTime, it chose an odd way to do it. The FaceTime app was pre-loaded onto AT&T devices when sold, a step hardly designed to impede use. Moreover, AT&T itself was selling no product in competition to FaceTime, leaving it little motive to block it. But AT&T and its customers did have a real interest in protecting users from congestion caused by the FaceTime application.

Verizon, AT&T's main competitor, made a different decision, allowing unconditional FaceTime use (and giving consumers a choice). Within a year, AT&T had dropped its restrictions as well, also without FCC interference.

Quashing New Competition: Google Fiber. Google, long one of the staunchest supporters of net neutrality rules, has itself been accused of violating those rules. The case involved Google Fiber, a broadband ISP run by Google. Under the terms of service issued by Google Fiber, subscribers were not to run "servers" on Google Fiber connections. Google Fiber, the company explained, was intended as a consumer service, not a business service. Still, a consumer in Kansas filed a complaint

No to Net Neutrality

Internet bandwidth is . . . a finite resource and has to be allocated somehow. We can let politicians decide, or we can let you and me decide by leaving it up to the free market. If we choose politicians, we will see the Internet become another mismanaged public monopoly, subject to political whims and increased scrutiny from our friends at the NSA [National Security Agency]. If we leave it up to the free market, we will . . . receive more of what we want at a lower price.

Josh Steimle,
"Am I the Only Techie Against Net Neutrality?,"
Forbes, May 14, 2014.

against Google with the FCC, citing the neutrality rules' ban on blocking "non-harmful devices."

Google Fiber is a new entrant into the ISP marketplace. It is a major initiative by Google, intended to challenge the major incumbent broadband providers by creating a new competitor to their networks.

The complaint posed an obstacle to this pro-consumer effort. But rather than reduce unnecessary barriers to this welcome competition, the FCC's interference would simply have added another barrier. And, given Google's total lack of market power in this marketplace, there was no plausible benefit for consumers.

Google's response to the FCC on the matter argued that the server ban was "reasonable network management," exempt from regulation. The FCC took no further action: Google Fiber has since continued to expand, challenging the leading ISPs in a small but growing number of cities.

Making the Consumer Pay: AT&T and Sponsored Data. In January, just weeks before the FCC's neutrality rule was overturned, AT&T unveiled an innovative pricing plan for wireless services known as "sponsored data." The idea is simple—participating content providers would pick up any data charges incurred by consumers when using their sites. By freeing potential users from the risk of exceeding their data caps and being hit with additional charges, the plan encourages them to spend more time on each site.

For instance, the ESPN sports network has been trying to build up its online offerings in a bid to create an alternative to traditional cable TV systems in the delivery of sports programs. One major concern of ESPN strategists is that viewers may balk, not knowing whether watching their favorite teams online would put them over their data cap and end up costing them a fortune in excess use charges. Under a sponsored data plan, that risk would be covered by ESPN, not the consumer. It would be like offering 800 numbers for the web, with content providers paying the cost of connection, but getting more business in return.

But the idea set off alarm bells in the net neutrality community. When ESPN was reported to be considering a similar deal with Verizon last year, pro-regulation groups immediately cried foul, with one posting a commentary titled: "This Is What a Net Neutrality Violation Looks Like."

They were wrong. Since it only applies to wireless service, the plan never ran afoul of net neutrality limits. Even more important, the proposed system is good for consumers, who pay less for more, and for businesses on the web, who generate more traffic. Such arrangements are common and beneficial marketplace tools—especially when new services and technologies are involved.

Net neutrality advocates still fret that the plan will disadvantage some firms. According to Free Press policy director Matt Wood:

Content and app providers that can't pay this new toll to reach customers will be at a huge disadvantage, and may never get off the ground in the first place if they can't afford AT&T's sponsor fees. Letting the carriers charge more or less money to reach certain sites is discriminatory, and it's not how the Internet is supposed to work.

But there is no new toll here—websites are merely providing a discount for consumers.

Some content providers will be able to match them, others not. That is exactly how a marketplace, and the Internet, is supposed to work, and hardly justifies regulation.

Next Steps

The federal appeals court decision will not end the long-running debate over net neutrality. To the contrary, it will likely signal a new round of activity. Proposals are already being introduced in Congress to restore the rules. Such legislation will face an uphill fight—in fact, in 2011, the House of Representatives passed legislation to *overturn* the regulation. But eventual passage of the legislation cannot be ruled out.

The most likely neutrality battleground, however, is—once again—the FCC. The court's opinion, in fact, all but invited the FCC to take another shot at imposing net neutrality rules. Despite its rejection of the regulation as written, the court did find that the agency had general power to regulate broadband Internet service. Thus, although the specific rules did not pass muster, other forms of regulation could be upheld. No doubt with this in mind, Tom Wheeler, the FCC's chairman, has already stated that the agency will "revisit" the neutrality issue.

Opponents of FCC neutrality regulation could also take the initiative, with legislation to reverse the court's ruling on broad regulatory powers. This would also be an uphill fight, but would close a potentially dangerous avenue for new regulation.

Conclusion

Consumers should cheer the recent appeals court decision voiding the FCC's net neutrality rules. Despite the Chicken Little claims of its supporters, broadband consumers were hurt, not helped, by the agency's restrictions. Rather than guarding against market abuses by dominant firms, the rules have been invoked in attempts to hinder innovation, impede competition, and block consumer price protections. Policy makers in Congress and at the FCC should not restore these unnecessary and harmful regulations.

> *"The Obama administration is showing confidence in the global community and in its ability to shield the Internet from repressive governments or excessive governmental control."*

Global Cooperation Is Key to Internet Governance

Lynn St. Amour and Don Tapscott

In the following viewpoint, Lynn St. Amour and Don Tapscott argue in favor of establishing global governance of the Internet. In describing an April 2014 NETmundial meeting in Brazil, the authors make the argument that global Internet governance will be a necessity moving forward and that the United States should cede more of its control of the Internet as the world's global communications needs and concerns grow and evolve. St. Amour is the president and chief executive officer of Internet Matters, an online safety organization. Tapscott is an author and Internet consultant who has penned such works as Macrowikinomics: New Solutions for a Connected Planet.

As you read, consider the following questions:

1. According to the authors, how does the Internet's success to this point suggest the potential for global governance to succeed in turn?

Lynn St. Amour and Don Tapscott, "The Way We Govern the Internet Is a Model in International Cooperation," HuffingtonPost.com, April 29, 2014. © 2014 Huffington Post. Reproduced by permission.

2. According to the viewpoint, why is global Internet governance a necessity?

3. According to the authors, why is a road map for the future evolution of Internet governance important?

Last week [in April 2014] in Brazil, thousands of interested parties met to thrash out the future development of Internet governance. Brazil hosted the NETmundial congress in response to the revelations that the U.S. government has been carrying out mass surveillance not only of its own citizens but also of foreign government leaders, which incensed Brazilian president Dilma Rousseff.

The meeting's success shows how the Internet enables new partnerships to grapple with difficult issues facing the world.

One of the most advanced examples is the ecosystem that governs the Internet itself—a diverse and global collection of individuals, nongovernmental organizations [NGOs], companies, interest groups, academics and governmental organizations. No one government, corporation or state-based institution controls the Internet, yet it has achieved stunning growth and reliability.

The Brazil meeting had a daunting list of objectives. The prime goal was to adopt a set of Internet governance principles and develop a road map for the future evolution of Internet governance.... Despite contentious issues such as the human rights language and net neutrality, the meeting achieved broad consensus. A reading of the final document was met with an emotional standing ovation from the audience, particularly after the principles and human rights section.

The Move Toward Global Governance

So far, the Internet community has focused largely on the technical standards required for this unprecedented communications medium to work. This success was reflected in last

Road Map for the Future of the Internet

The Internet governance framework is a distributed and coordinated ecosystem involving various organizations and fora. It must be inclusive, transparent and accountable, and its structures and operations must follow an approach that enables the participation of all stakeholders in order to address the interests of all those who use the Internet as well as those who are not yet online. . . .

Internet governance should promote sustainable and inclusive development. . . . Participation should reflect geographic diversity and include stakeholders from developing [and] least developed countries and small island developing states.

"NETmundial Multistakeholder Statement,"
NETmundial, April 24, 2014.

month's announcement that the U.S. government was going to hand over key technical elements of the Internet to a "global multi-stakeholder community."

By indicating that it is willing to relinquish the few remaining vestiges of American control over the Internet, the [Barack] Obama administration is showing confidence in the global community and in its ability to shield the Internet from repressive governments or excessive governmental control.

Some U.S. Republicans, including former Alaska governor Sarah Palin, denounced the move, saying it was the Obama administration's equivalent of former U.S. president Jimmy Carter's decision to give away the Panama Canal. But such criticism is misguided. The multi-stakeholder Internet governance ecosystem has been enormously effective in supporting the Internet's rapid development, and has demonstrated great agility and determination to protect the net as a truly global open resource.

But as the Brazil conference showed, Internet governance is entering a new phase. As this digital tool penetrates and alters every aspect of economic, social and political life, there are more profound and broad nontechnical questions that must be addressed. These include thorny policy issues ranging from privacy, security and neutrality of the net to spam, pornography and intellectual property.

The Meeting

To respond to these issues, the Internet's stewards wanted to articulate clearly the principles upon which their decisions are based. In the run-up to Brazil, the meeting's organizers experimented with an innovative process. The meeting was preceded by an online public consultation of a draft outcome document prepared by the "executive multi-stakeholder committee" comprising representatives from across key sectors, such as civil society, the private sector, the technical community, academia and governments. The review of the document continued during the meeting itself through a quite lengthy series of interventions all commenting on the draft document.

The primary basis for the document was a statement on human rights and shared values and this was widely, but not universally, supported. The final document states: "Human rights are universal as reflected in the Universal Declaration of Human Rights and that should underpin Internet governance principles. Rights that people have off-line must also be protected online."

Mass surveillance was the hottest single issue, and the final document included a clause saying the right to privacy means freedom from arbitrary and unlawful surveillance. The group could not agree on a second hot issue—net neutrality—the idea that Internet service providers [ISPs] should treat all data on the Internet equally, not discriminating or charging different fees because of the nature of the data or its source.

The second part of the agreement was the road map for the future evolution of Internet governance. This will be enormously helpful, as the road ahead will surely be bumpy. It's one thing for this community to agree on global standards for an effective and smooth-running Internet. It's another for everyone to agree on the tougher policy issues where players have differing cultural and economic interests. Storm warnings came from Russia, India and Cuba who insisted on having reservations read into the record of the meeting.

A Hopeful Outlook

Unlike the UN [United Nations] or other government-based bodies, these are less formal communities. They come together to govern over this global public resource and function more on collaboration, merit and consensus. In this spirit, the NETmundial results were a statement of consensus, and while nonbinding, one can safely expect governments, companies and NGOs around the world to take heed.

As NETmundial says, this meeting "represents the beginning of a process for the construction of such policies in the global context, following a model of participatory plurality."

Every country needs to consider a bill of rights for the digital age, and the meeting has already catalyzed a wave of global activity to ensure that governments, corporations and others do the right thing.

"Ceding oversight over what can go on the web to countries like China and Russia, countries not known for their open attitude toward information, would fundamentally change the way the Internet operates."

Global Governance Is a Threat to Open Internet

Peter Roff

In the following viewpoint, Peter Roff argues that the United States should not acquiesce to foreign demands for the establishment of global Internet governance. He asserts that doing so would seriously jeopardize the freedoms afforded by the Internet and make cyberspace a far more dangerous environment for users. Roff is an on-air policy analyst with One America News Network *and a former senior political writer for* United Press International.

As you read, consider the following questions:

1. According to Roff, why would global Internet governance pose a threat to online freedoms?

2. How would global Internet governance make the Internet more dangerous for users, according to the viewpoint?

3. How does Roff suggest the US government should respond to the question of global Internet governance?

The evolution of the Internet has not only changed the world of commerce; it's revolutionized the diplomatic sphere and helped democratize the foreign policy process.

Up until the end of the 20th century, the United States relied heavily on human intelligence to learn the truth about what was happening inside countries that had closed themselves off to the rest of the world. The Internet's penetration of even the most authoritarian of nations has created a window through which the U.S. and the other democratic nations that make up the first world can see for themselves what is going on.

It is through the Internet that America has been able to follow the story unfolding inside Iran, and it is the Internet through which the Western powers were able to confirm that the [Bashar al-]Assad regime in Syria both had chemical weapons and had used them against opponents of the government. There was no need to wait for a group of inspectors working on behalf of a global body to confirm the allegations. With the web, the world could see with its own eyes just what had occurred.

The Globalization of Internet Governance

The democratization of information, which is a powerful tool for keeping the peace, is imperiled by the [Barack] Obama administration's refusal to resist demands from the International Telecommunication Union, the European Union, Brazil, Russia, China, and other countries to become stakeholders in the process of Internet governance.

In fact plans may already be under way to do just that. No one has yet announced what the United States might have agreed to at a late February [2014] meeting in Barcelona, called as a sidebar to the Mobile World [Congress]. The gathering was organized by the Brazilians to "advance proposals and streamline details for the agenda of the Global Multistakeholder Meeting on the Future of Internet Governance, to be held in São Paulo on April 23." Brazil has been a global champion of the idea that the oversight of the Internet needs to be broadened and that the United States currently has too much to say about it.

The idea of broadened authority has its critics however.

"It is urgent that the federal government and U.S. private sector vigorously oppose all efforts to try and take away U.S.-centered controls over the Internet," Flash/Critic Cyber Threat News publisher Bill Gertz said.

"Current proposals for Internet governance call for controlling and routing Internet traffic and reviewing content for potential censorship," Gertz continued. "This would threaten press freedom at a time when democratic forces are widely using the Internet to promote fundamental freedoms against tyranny."

The Problem with Global Internet Governance

Ceding oversight over what can go on the web to countries like China and Russia, countries not known for their open attitude toward information, would fundamentally change the way the Internet operates. Instead of being a window on the activities of the world, it could be made to function as an extension of state news services that are more concerned with perpetuating cover stories than with exposing the truth. In a very profound way, our respect for free speech, free assembly and, where the net is concerned, free and open access is strategically important to U.S. national security.

"Clearly there is a danger of significant censorship of political speech on the Internet if nations without fidelity to our Bill of Rights are permitted to impose their values on what is permissible criticism and debate," former House science committee chairman Bob Walker said. "We should not kid ourselves about that danger when we have seen some of the grossest international violators of human rights given seats on international human rights panels."

Likewise, the establishment of global protocols by a worldwide body—as opposed to those generated primarily within the United States and influenced by American values—would make the World Wide Web more of a hacker's paradise than it is today, further jeopardizing U.S. national security interests.

Giving up control of Internet governance to a global body "would undermine U.S. national security by increasing cyberespionage opportunities for adversaries like Russia, China and Iran," Gertz said.

"It also would increase the risk that foreign states with advanced cyber-attack capabilities will find it easier to conduct cyber-reconnaissance—what the military calls preparation of the battle space for a future conflict that will involve strategic cyber-attacks on critical infrastructures, like electrical grids, financial networks and communications and transportation infrastructures."

The potential dangers are very real. The Obama White House's lackadaisical response to the demands by other countries that the structure of Internet governance be changed is yet another example of its overall weakness in foreign policy. The president has already demonstrated his willingness to give up things that are in the United States' best interests in pursuit of favorable poll numbers overseas.

This is a foolish, even dangerous, trade-off. Congress should intervene to make sure that oversight of the web's functionality remains primarily an American job.

Periodical and Internet Sources Bibliography

The following articles have been selected to supplement the diverse views presented in this chapter.

Leonymae Aumentado	"NETmundial: Steps Towards Global Internet Governance," *Diplomatic Courier*, November 28, 2014.
Vinton G. Cerf	"Internet Access Is Not a Human Right," *New York Times*, January 4, 2012.
Jeffrey Dorfman	"Net Neutrality Is a Bad Idea Supported by Poor Analogies," *Forbes*, November 13, 2014.
The Economist	"Doing the ICANN-can," March 22, 2014.
Scott Edwards	"Is Internet Access a Human Right?," Amnesty International, January 10, 2012.
Julius Genachowski	"'Global' Internet Government Invites Censorship," *Wall Street Journal*, April 3, 2014.
Michael Joseph Gross	"World War 3.0," *Vanity Fair*, May 2012.
Mike Montgomery	"US Must Take Net Neutrality Seriously," *The Hill*, August 11, 2015.
Adam Wagner	"Is Internet Access a Human Right?," *Guardian*, January 11, 2012.
Matt Walsh	"Dear Foolish and Gullible Americans, Net Neutrality Is Not Your Friend," The Blaze, February 27, 2015.
Steve Wozniak	"Steve Wozniak to the FCC: Keep the Internet Free," *Atlantic*, December 21, 2010.
Tim Wu	"Net Neutrality: How the Government Finally Got It Right," *New Yorker*, February 5, 2015.

OPPOSING
VIEWPOINTS®
SERIES

CHAPTER 2

How Does the Internet Impact the World?

Chapter Preface

Since the time of its inception, the Internet has assumed a larger and ever more invasive role in daily life. Where once Internet access was a rare commodity, it has now, in the modern world, become a commonplace service that individuals often expect to be available practically everywhere at all times. As the Internet has evolved, so too have the ways people interact with it and the ways they have integrated it into their lives. That evolution ultimately led to the information age, a modern era in which high-speed Internet and cutting-edge communications technology have connected people around the globe and left the world a smaller place than ever before. As this evolution continues, however, society finds itself in the midst of a digital debate between those who believe it will lead to an even better future and those who believe it will lead only to dystopia.

In recent years, experts have expended considerable time and energy studying the social effects of the Internet and the increased connectedness it has made possible. Regardless of whether those effects are ultimately deemed negative or positive, it is clear that they have been significant. Society is becoming increasingly "me-centric," or focused more on the individual than the larger community. While the concept of community certainly still exists, the definition of community is now determined less by geography and face-to-face relationships and more by individual interests shared with others through cyberspace. A major reason for this shift is the rise of social networking.

Social networking websites, such as Facebook, Twitter, and Instagram, allow users to connect with people from around the world and share their thoughts, likes, dislikes, and whatever else they so choose. Through social media, people can now forge and maintain online relationships with friends, family members, and even complete strangers they may never actually meet in real life. As social media has become increasingly popular, many have noted its obvious impact on society. While some argue that it erodes real-life relationships and leads to an unhealthy degree of social isolation, others contend that it actually makes real-life relationships stronger and encourages people to be more socially active than they otherwise would be. With the Internet and social media constantly becoming a bigger part of people's lives, this debate is sure to continue for years to come.

The ongoing debate over social media, however, is only one part of the discussion as to how the Internet is shaping modern society. Similar debates are also unfolding over how the Internet is affecting journalism, education, and more. Looking toward the future, the discussion also encompasses the question of just how far individuals should allow the Internet to be integrated into their lives moving forward. In that realm, somewhat experimental concepts such as the Internet of Things, or the effort to connect all devices to the Internet and to each other, are among the most hot-button issues. However the Internet evolves from here, it will undoubtedly play a significant role in the continuing evolution of modern society.

The following chapter further explores the concept of the Internet of Things and how the Internet impacts the world around us.

> *"By some measures, journalism has never been healthier. And there's every reason to believe that it is actually getting stronger because of the web, not weaker—regardless of what's happening to print."*

The Internet Has Not Been Detrimental to Journalism

Mathew Ingram

In the following viewpoint, Mathew Ingram argues that the Internet, contrary to popular belief, has actually been beneficial for journalism. He contends that despite its apparently deleterious effect on the traditional media industry, the Internet is actually strengthening and improving the art of journalism itself. Ingram is an award-winning senior writer with Gigaom who covers media and web culture. Previously, he served as a writer for the Globe and Mail, *a Toronto-based newspaper.*

As you read, consider the following questions:

1. Why does Ingram reject critics' concerns about too many online journalists being willing to write for free?

2. According to Ingram, why does it not matter if new media entities do not employ enough people to make up for the loss of jobs in the traditional media marketplace?

Mathew Ingram, "Journalism Is Doing Just Fine, Thanks—It's Mass-Media Business Models That Are Ailing," Gigaom, August 26, 2014. Reproduced by permission.

3. According to Ingram, why is the Internet an ideal environment for journalism to flourish?

Is the Internet destroying journalism? In a piece at Salon, writer Andrew Leonard argues that it is—primarily because "the economics of news gathering in the Internet age suck," as he puts it. And it's easy to see why someone would be drawn to that point of view, given the rapid decline of the print newspaper business and the waves of layoffs and closures that have affected that industry. But what Leonard is actually complaining about is the failure of a specific business model for funding journalism, not the decline of journalism itself.

Obviously, those two things are fairly closely related: Newspapers have represented the front lines of journalism for a generation or more, with deep benches of talent—including foreign correspondents in dozens of countries around the world, and special investigative reporting teams. And what has funded all of that journalism has been print advertising revenue, which has been falling off a cliff for the past decade or two: Since 2000, more than $45 billion worth of revenue has effectively disappeared from the print newspaper business.

But while journalism and the print newspaper or print magazine industry have close ties to one another, and have since the 1950s or so, that doesn't mean they are synonymous, or that because one is fatally ill the other must necessarily die. In fact, by some measures, journalism has never been healthier. And there's every reason to believe that it is actually getting stronger because of the web, not weaker—regardless of what's happening to print.

Journalism Is More than Just Newspapers

Even Leonard admits that surveys repeatedly show people are reading more news than they ever have before, thanks in large part to the rise of mobile devices, and he agrees that the worst of the SEO [search engine optimization]–driven content farms have been vanquished. He also notes that a lot of money has been flowing into online content over the past year, including Amazon CEO [chief executive officer] Jeff Bezos buying the *Washington Post* for $250 million, eBay founder Pierre Omidyar funding First Look Media for a similar amount, and close to $100 million flowing to BuzzFeed and Vox.

One thing we know for sure: People still want to read the news, and where there is demand there will always be supply. And certainly, if you are a reader, you already are flourishing in a golden age, with access to more content of all kinds than you can possibly consume.

So if readers are being well served, and news reading has never been more popular, then why should we be concerned about the future of journalism? Leonard argues that while readers are getting what they want, "a golden age for readers doesn't necessarily translate into a golden age for writers or publishers." For one thing, he says, writers are having a hard time making a living because too many people are willing to work for free—a complaint about the Internet's effect on the media industry that comes up from time to time.

Whenever I write about this subject, I get deluged by flame e-mails and Twitter responses, but I don't see how more people writing journalism—even for free—is a problem. If what we care about is the future of journalism, then it's actually a good thing, not a bad thing: The more people doing journalism, the better it gets. What Leonard seems concerned about is a particular economic model for producing and distributing that journalism. But who's to say that the model whose death we are mourning was any better than a new or different model? Here's Leonard again:

> Yes, there are a handful of high-profile start-ups making waves, but it's not at all clear that they've replaced the hundreds and thousands of metro and foreign desk reporter jobs that have vanished in the last decade. . . . One 2011

Journalism and the Internet

The fact is that there was no "golden age of journalism." Journalism has always been a messy and chaotic and venal undertaking in many ways.... All the web has done is provide us with more ways to produce and distribute both ephemeral nonsense and serious journalism in greater quantities.

Mathew Ingram,
"Journalism and the Internet: Is It the Best of Times?
No—but It's Not the Worst of Times Either,"
Gigaom, August 28, 2014.

study found 44.7 percent fewer reporters working in the [San Francisco] Bay area than a decade ago.

The Economics Have Never Been Better

Here's the question implied by Leonard's argument: Should the Internet, or new media entities like BuzzFeed or Vice or Vox, be judged by whether they have been able to replace the thousands of reporter and editor jobs that have vanished in the last decade? I don't think they should. That would be a little like judging the early years of the automotive industry based on how many horse- or buggy-whip-related jobs it managed to replace. Obviously, Vice and Vox and First Look are not going to reconstruct the kind of print-based news industry that ruled the mass media world of the 1950s and 1960s. But then why should they?

But for me, the most problematic sentence in Leonard's piece is the one where he says that "the economics of news gathering in the Internet age suck." That couldn't be further from the truth. As Henry Blodget of Business Insider argued in a post last year [2013] about why we are living in a golden age for journalism, the benefits of newsgathering and distribution in a digital age are numerous, and they arguably make both of those functions cheaper by orders of magnitude—to the point where many of the jobs Leonard is mourning are simply not needed any more.

Is the transition from an old model to a new one causing horrendous economic upheaval? Of course it is. And it's not easy for editors or reporters or writers of any kind to make the transition from one way of doing things to another—but it can be done, and it will be done. And journalism will be just fine, even if print-based newspapers and magazines are not.

> "New tools should be scrutinized intensely and skeptically, as should the people who stand to gain vast new forms of power and wealth when they are widely adopted. That didn't happen with journalism and the Internet, and now we're paying the price."

The Internet Has Been Detrimental for Journalism

David Sessions

In the following viewpoint, David Sessions argues that the Internet has had an overall detrimental effect on journalism. He contends that Internet journalism, though it far outpaces traditional journalism in terms of quantity, provides little in the way of quality. This lack of quality reporting, he says, is systematically eroding journalistic integrity. Sessions is the founding editor of Patrol *and a contributor to other media outlets such as* Newsweek, Slate, *and the* Daily Beast.

As you read, consider the following questions:

1. According to Sessions, why is the Internet bad for writers?

David Sessions, "The State of the Internet Is Awful, and Everybody Knows It," Patrol Mag.com, August 25, 2014. © 2014 Patrol Magazine. Reproduced by permission.

2. According to Sessions, why is the Internet bad for readers?

3. How might the Internet still be valuable for journalists, according to the viewpoint?

I began my media career about seven years ago as an unabashed Internet enthusiast. As I've said before, I never worked in print journalism and had little nostalgia for the world that was entering free fall as I did my first internship at an online publication. By then, the Internet had already provided me an outlet for various creative pursuits for years, and I saw nothing but the opportunity to escape some of traditional journalism's worst constraints, which were related both to the print medium and to the sorts of gatekeepers and ideologies that controlled it. I never read print newspapers or magazines devotedly, so I never experienced unsettling changes in habits the way many people have as they transitioned primarily to digital reading in the past decade. Blogs and start-up web publications were always much more to my taste than "old media"; their immediacy, their freedom, and their ability to evolve and adapt quickly always seemed promising and exciting.

Things look a lot different now. The Internet won, and despite killing off thousands of jobs in the print industry, it created many more than expected in an ever-multiplying array of new web ventures. But now that it won, it's increasingly unclear that was a good thing. A lot of people who work in Internet media secretly—or in many cases, not so secretly—hate it, and some even suspect they are actively making the world a dumber place, as they very well may be. (I was one of them, which is a big part of why I decided to quit.) Good writing and journalism have not gone extinct, but have been reduced to sharing an undifferentiated plane with lots of cynical, unnecessary, mind-numbing, time-wasting "content," much of which hardly qualifies as writing at all. The *New York Times* and ViralNova look exactly the same in your Facebook feed. As a result, journalism that once had a certain amount of aesthetic self-respect, even online, now has little choice but to mimic the shameless pandering of advertising-driven "content." Where once the Internet media landscape was populated with publications that all had unique visual styles, traffic models, and editorial voices, each one has mission creeped its way into a version of the same thing: Everybody has to cover everything, regardless of whether or not they can add any value to the story, and has to scream at you to stand out in the avalanche of "content" gushing out of your feeds.

This is not "the Internet's" fault; the Internet, after all, is not a thing; it's a complex tangle of things that people made and change all the time. As Evgeny Morozov constantly points out, the Internet is not a force of nature with a will of its own; people control it, fight over it, and decide what it is. It is a for-profit business. Most of the horrible features of the current iteration of the Internet media I just described are the result of decisions made by two major Internet power brokers, Google and Facebook. The mistake media people made early on was to assume that the Internet had laws that had to be obeyed even at high costs to their work, and—as is so depressingly typical of human history—that new ways of doing things were superior simply because they were possible. Once it was clear that the "disruption" of journalism could not be stopped, the media became the Internet's most eager, least critical stenographers and early adopters, lapping up every development that remapped the media landscape on a nearly yearly basis. It was partly in journalism's racing, competitive spirit to do so, but partly out of sheer terror at the possibility being left behind. Now that Internet media is at the front of the Internet curve—or at least doing pretty well at keeping up—they've made it their job to become the unpaid PR [public relations] machine of Silicon Valley and the self-appointed mockers of all who resist "disruption" wherever the latest 20-year-old billionaire has decided to inflict it.

The Price of Internet Journalism

The social consequences of this enormous change are hard even to fathom, much less analyze; the consequences have affected labor, privacy, interpersonal ethics, and virtually every sector of the modern economy. As plenty of others have noted before, the relative lack of deliberation and consideration that have accompanied the shift—the degree to which it is simply assumed to be positive and benevolent—should be shocking and alarming. But since my subject here is journalism, I'll simply focus on that as an example. There is very little evidence the enormous effort invested to keep Internet media up to date with the latest tech trends has changed much for the better. The media itself is inside a reality-distortion field where ever-increasing speed and fragmentation are somehow seen as positive. But take a single step outside it and the picture changes drastically. Delete one of your social media accounts, or simply go on vacation for a week, and you will be shocked how little any of it matters. For most people most of the time, flipping through a newspaper once a day—even once a week—is enough to provide a basic level of information about what's going on the in the world, little of which affects them anyhow. But the Internet media now operates as if its mission is to provide 24-hour infotainment. I honestly believe their time would be better spent reading books, watching movies, or spending time with their friends and family than "consuming" "content" from "social." In case you're wondering, that is how the people who make their money throwing "content" at you talk about it.

Even in a breaking news event, the instantaneous "coverage" now provided by the Internet media generally proves to be substantially worthless. The much-analyzed night the Boston Marathon bombers were arrested is an instructive example: Every detail was followed for hours on Twitter, while countless false reports were amplified by major media outlets, innocent people were blamed for things they didn't do, etc. *Absolutely nothing* worthwhile—nothing social, political, moral, personally enriching—was achieved by the way that night was covered online. If breaking news coverage is supposed to be hours-long, anxiety-inducing interactive entertainment, then it was great. If you simply wanted a truthful account of what happened, a reported, verified, and synthesized account printed in a newspaper a couple of days later was a much better option. All that the Internet media, with its celebrated news reporting tools provided, was a lot of wasted hours trying to piece through false information about something you had no pressing need to know in the first place. (That said, I do think there's a distinction between media-led voyeurism like the Boston bomber manhunt and other times that important events, like the Ferguson protests [referring to protests in Ferguson, Missouri, that broke out after an unarmed black teenager was shot and killed by a white police officer], have become stories after they bubbled up organically through social media.)

When the Internet first reared its cheeky head, the old guard acted like incurious old people do, like they could just tune out the newfangled stuff and go on about their business. But now that nearly the entire old guard has converted to techno-utopians, anyone who tries to mount a criticism of Internet-ism is mercilessly mocked as an out-of-touch fogey saying the same old thing, even though we now have several years of experience by which to assess that critique. Seven years ago, I probably would have mocked John MacArthur, the publisher of *Harper's*, the way a lot of media insiders did a few weeks ago when this article about his insistence on print ran. This is how the *Times* summarized his views:

> His thesis is built on three pillars. The web is bad for writers, he said, who are too exhausted by the pace of an endless

news cycle to write poised, reflective stories and who are paid peanuts if they do. It's bad for publishers, who have lost advertising revenue to Google and Facebook and will never make enough from a free model to sustain great writing. And it's bad for readers, who cannot absorb information well on devices that buzz, flash and generally distract.

As a writer, editor, and reader, I now agree with every word of that. In various professional capacities I've had to assign articles that needed to be turned around in a matter of hours just to "have something on it," even though fifteen other sites had already published nearly identical articles. Those instances were a tacit admission that quality is secondary to keeping up with the pack. They were an insult to writers (asking them to produce work that cannot possibly be worth a reader's time) and, above all, an insult to the people we expect to read what we publish. The Internet is bad for writers because it turns qualities that should be valued—effort, reflection, revision, editing—into hindrances, and makes the resulting product worth little, both qualitatively and financially. Good writing, writing that matters in the present and is remembered in the future, is very difficult, takes a lot of time, and is generally expensive. It takes isolation and focus. Ta-Nehisi Coates didn't write "The Case for Reparations" in time to post before the morning newsletter went out.

The Internet is bad for readers not just because the devices on which they access it divide their attention and intensify the effort required to read anything at all, but because it enables—even demands—the overproduction of worthless material that is difficult to distinguish online from quality work. Quality work is institutionally devalued, and what still does manage to get produced has to compete in flat, featureless spaces that deliberately eliminate the indicators physical mediums have traditionally used to distinguish and prioritize reading material. And even if the reader can be roused from their feed-induced trance enough to click, there is little point

Bad News for Journalism

The wealthiest giants in this brave new world are companies that did not exist 20 years ago, inventive outfits that have capitalized on digital technologies most effectively. Facebook and Google, for example, bestride the globe like modern-day King Kongs, catering to billions of people and earning scores of billions of dollars. Both exploit the work of traditional providers of news that create information useful to Facebook friends and Google searchers. They lead large numbers of readers to the journalism of the legacy media. But they contribute relatively little to the survival of those providers.

These firms were created by a new generation of young people whose self-interest may lead them either to realize the importance of the legacy institutions, or figure out how to create new ways to do what the old news organizations did in the past. Financially, it would be easy for Google to rescue the *New York Times*. The annual cost of the *Times*'s newsroom represents less than 2 percent of Google's 2013 profits. Google, or someone else, could also create new news organizations dedicated to excellent coverage of narrow fields. The future, in Mort Sahl's wise words, lies ahead—but remains invisible.

News as we know it is at risk. So is democratic governance, which depends on an effective watchdog news media. Both have been undermined by changes in society wrought by digital technologies—among the most powerful forces ever unleashed by mankind. We have barely begun the digital age, and there is no point in trying to predict just where it will take us. News certainly has a future, but what that will be is unclear.

Robert G. Kaiser, "The Bad News About the News,"
Brookings Institution, October 16, 2014.

in actually reading anything, because so much of it exists simply to produce the act of clicking. A vast majority of the time, the actual *writing* is indistinguishable from what is on every other site, and if it's any different, it's only different in a cynical effort to bring a different angle to the problem of everybody else's angle on the problem. (In my experience, when editors say quality is what distinguishes their site, it is not because that is actually the case; it is because at some level they realize nothing does.) Readers aren't stupid, so they sift instead of read; even if they have good intentions of "reading it later," the Instapaper and Pocket [referring to applications that allow users to save web articles for later reading] pile up and overflow, rarely touched. As Choire Sicha put it earlier this year [2014]:

> I do not read a lot of things anymore. A lot of us don't, we sort of go where the tide takes us. I feel weird about that. I opened up my Digg reader the other day, because I was on blogging duty at work, and everything was so duplicative of each other. I was like, yeah, okay, there's that piece of news filtering through all these different websites, all the same things . . . no wonder I don't go to them. I need to make a new folder in my Digg reader, I guess, that's "Things That Are Surprising and Interesting and Maybe Weird." It's sort of . . . it's not . . . I don't know, something's wrong.

The Future of Journalism

Something's wrong. I've been convinced of it for quite a while, and so are a lot of other people who can't say it because they have to pay their rent somehow. So much of it is stupid and worthless, and everybody knows it. And worse, so many people in other off-line sectors of society think that what happens in the Internet media is the future for their industry, and should be emulated and brought in to "disrupt" things so they won't be left behind, too. People in Internet media love to cultivate that, because honestly, who doesn't want to be thought of as blazing the trail into the bright future?

This has been a negative post, and for good reason. But none of my hostility to what now passes for Internet journalism means that "the Internet is bad" or "print was better" or that Internet media should be universally condemned and older forms of accessing reporting and writing championed. Absolutely nothing of the sort. I still believe there are parts of journalism, even when they happen in different ways in new mediums, that are a crucial part of a healthy society. I am still glad the Internet brought into existence the tools it has for writing, research, and reaching an audience. In general, I'm happy a lot more things see the light of day than they used to, and a lot more criticism and argument about every subject under the sun gets read and participated in, even if a lot of that argument is about ridiculous, bullshit things that don't matter. The point, rather, is that *tools are just tools, and just as they are not bad because they might change things, they are not good just because they are new and available.* New tools should be scrutinized intensely and skeptically, as should the people who stand to gain vast new forms of power and wealth when they are widely adopted. That didn't happen with journalism and the Internet, and now we're paying the price.

> "*Imagine a future where a chipped-up Coke can connects to your smart watch, confirms your identity, and automatically adds bonus points to your balance as some sort of rewards program.*"

Why We're (Beyond) Geeked for the Internet of Things

Evan Wade

In the following viewpoint, Evan Wade reports that the Internet of Things (IoT), or the effort to connect all devices to the Internet and to each other, has the potential to be tremendously beneficial in the years to come. He provides several examples to show how the technology is being utilized today, including a lock that allows users to unlock doors using smartphones or personal computers, and speculates where advances may occur. Wade says that the technology is in the beginning stages, but he is hopeful for the future possibilities electronic connectivity can offer. Wade is a writer and journalist.

As you read, consider the following questions:

1. According to Wade, what factors contribute to the backbone of the Internet of Things?

Evan Wade, "Why We're (Beyond) Geeked for the Internet of Things," Techly, June 24, 2014. Reproduced by permission.

2. According to Wade, what are some of the things already working online?

3. What might a guitar connected through the Internet of Things be able to do, according to Wade?

It's easy to look at the term *Internet of Things* and cringe. Here we have what sounds like the quintessential tech industry buzz phrase, the kind of sorta-techie, sorta-cutesy bastardisation of language your average middle manager would love to latch onto and use approximately .6 times per sentence, "Hey, Mark, could you leverage the Internet of Things to reach out and get some leads before the close of play?"

As vacuous and abusable as it may sound, however, the phrase carries serious implications. The kind of world-changing potential matched only by other burgeoning technologies like 3-D printing and self-driving cars.

It's a combination of haute-tech concepts, and an invitation to seriously rethink exactly what tech *is* in the digital age.

You might be thinking it's also an opportunity for low-rent futurologists to wax philosophical about their hobby of choice, but bear with me. I'd like to tell you about what ideas the term Internet of Things encompasses, what it'll mean for people across the globe, and where it might take us in the future.

I guarantee something that comes from the technology itself will have you scraping your jaw off the floor at some point in the very near future.

If you aren't impressed by the end, you can pin the blame directly on me.

Welcome to the IoT

Tech gets more expensive and less powerful. Those two attributes really make the computing world what it is: Without people to buy an electronic product, there's rarely funding to make it better, and if it doesn't improve, there are no people to buy it.

Throw in the fact that it tends to get smaller, too, and you have the backbone of the whole IoT.

Look at this thing HP created. Sure, it'll probably be expensive in its early incarnations, but all technology is. Past that, it has all the makings of a classic revolutionary gadget: It's tiny, it's insanely powerful, and it packs a whole bunch of functions—Reuters called it "a server, workstation, PC and phone"—into one tiny space.

It's also exactly the kind of technology we'll see making the Internet of Things come to life. Simply put, the IoT is a realisation of the future we see in sci-fi movies and Silicon Valley visionaries' predictions: a sort of hopped-up uber-network that lets most everything humans interact with connect to the Internet for added functionality.

Locks. Thermostats. Sprinklers and blinds and house pets. These are just a few things we've already got online—and the list is far from done growing.

Please note that 'connect to the Internet' doesn't have to mean 'go online' in the common sense. No, you won't be firing up Firefox on your shoe like some high-tech re-envisioning of *Dragnet* (though that would be pretty cool). Instead, IoT-connected items will use—are using—the net to make our lives easier, letting us connect to them remotely and pull statistics on pretty much anything imaginable from them, among other uses. Lots and lots of other uses.

Other advancements are also helping pave the way for a super-connected future. Intel's undoubtedly working hard to bring us processors even smaller and less expensive than the already-small, already-cheap Quark. The smaller and less expensive they get, the more cool stuff businesses and enterprising individuals will be able to create.

Imagine a future where a chipped-up Coke can connects to your smart watch, confirms your identity, and automatically adds bonus points to your balance as some sort of rewards program. In the rapid-paced context of technological advancement, a future where that's possible is far off—but *far* in tech terms means nothing. At the rate we're moving towards total IoT connectivity, we could reasonably expect to see something like it in less than ten years. Maybe less than five.

On the Horizon

We've been connecting more and more devices to the Internet since day one. This is largely because of the factors mentioned a few paragraphs back: People have been harbouring all kinds of crazy (and useful) ideas for years, but they haven't had the hardware to make them a reality until now.

As things continue to shrink and get cheaper, even crazier ideas will see the light of day.

We've all heard the story about the refrigerator that checks your home food inventory and sends you an e-mail when you're, say, running low on milk. This is just one of thousands of ideas that'll become tangible products thanks to the potential of the Internet of Things.

Let's say you're a novice guitar player. You'd like to pay for traditional lessons, but money is tight and work schedules are brutal. In the future, you might be able to practice your scales on an IoT-connected guitar, which would upload a recording of what you played and info about your finger positioning to an off-site computer. That, then, would analyse your performance, send back info telling you what you're doing well and where you need to improve, and compare that data against old reports dating back to when you first picked up the connected instrument.

Sound far-fetched? Look at gadgets like the Fitbit and think again—it's the same concept, only with a musical twist. The challenges inherent to creating such an instrument would be large, sure, but it's hard to say anything along those lines is impossible in this day and age, and it'll only get harder to say as technology progresses.

Some of the stuff we're already doing is pretty nuts. Look at the Proteus line of gadgets, which effectively turn your average pill into a full-scale health-reporting assistant, tracking stats and measuring vitals for patients in need of monitoring. Or the above-mentioned Goji lock, which lets you unlock your door with your smartphone *and* assign permanent or temporary keys to other devices (say, a friend's tablet, or a maintenance man's iPhone) from any web-connected PC.

We're approaching a sort of event horizon in the world of consumer gadgetry: one where the stats we record and the items we want to remotely control are only limited by the creativity of the people doing the building. It's often said that there'll never be another original idea. . . . I submit that, in maybe a decade, maybe less, we'll be drowning in them. But in a good way.

We could fill dozens of articles up with ideas about how the IoT might help us. Speculation is interesting, but it doesn't contribute a lot to the discussion. The biggest point behind all of this is simply that, given time, most of that hypothetical speculation *could* come true.

Look at what developers are able to do with the collection of cameras and touch screens and GPS monitors we call smartphones today: If a team of creative developers used those tools to create applications like Word Lens, which uses the camera to analyse an image and translate it on the screen in real time, the thought of similar minds and talents being able to connect quite literally anything to the Internet is enough to inspire awe in and of itself.

It's limitless potential in the best kind of way. Computers (local and off-site) working in tandem to make lots of things we never thought would be possible, well, possible. And unlike the flying cars and phaser guns of sci-fi past, it's so close you can almost taste it.

We can certainly see it, at any rate, and that's tantalising enough.

The Future, Connected

There are other uses for the IoT—countless uses in countless sectors, from manufacturing plants to office buildings to anywhere else ideas like data collection, remote login/control, and autonomous analysis are needed. That is to say, everywhere.

And while it may sound like the uses largely come down to just that—remote access and statistics—that's just the beginning. A million thinkers more creative than the one whose work you're reading will find uses for those two functions that will blow all of our minds.

Toss in associated developments like cloud computing (the same thing powering stuff like Siri and the guitar example up top), and you have a host of high-tech potentiators, each expanding the creative tools available to developers like score multipliers in a video game.

So yes, *Internet of Things* as a phrase sounds like just another pile of letters we're bound to be sick of hearing in the near future. But as a concept, it's an unfathomably exciting, unbelievably powerful collection of advancements, just waiting to blow our combined socks off.

Better than all that—it's close. Close enough that we're already implementing it in ways a lot of people (your author included) would have considered much further off even a decade ago.

Considering the leaps we've already seen, it's fair to say whatever comes next will be as surprising and useful as it is unbelievable. In an era where we're jaded enough to ask our phones where the next service station is, or what the weather will be like tomorrow, receive a vocalised answer without ever speaking to another human, and not take a split second to consider how amazing the exchange was, that's an incredible thing to think about.

For all the concerns this world faces, a future where it's impossible to be jaded by the gadgets we use—or one where we're jaded by things that come close to hitting Clarke's "indistinguishable from magic" benchmark—is beyond exciting.

As a confirmed gadgethead and lifelong lover of most anything with processing power, the thought of seeing what's to come is something worth living for. I'm excited enough to say that without a shred of embarrassment. Are you?

> *"The 'Internet of Things' stands a really good chance of turning into the 'Internet of unmaintained, insecure, and dangerously hackable things.'"*

The Internet of Things May Be Problematic

Peter Bright

In the following viewpoint, Peter Bright argues that the Internet of Things (IoT), or the effort to connect all devices to the Internet and to each other, is unlikely to be as beneficial as promised. Citing several different key examples, Bright says that the IoT is likely to be wrought with shortcomings that will almost certainly render it impractical, ineffective, and possibly even wasteful. Bright is the technology editor for Ars Technica and specializes in software development, programming, browsers, and more.

As you read, consider the following questions:

1. According to Bright, why will many smart devices connected through the Internet of Things be prone to security issues?

2. Why might the Internet of Things lead to wastefulness, according to the viewpoint?

3. According to Bright, what will manufacturers have to do to make the Internet of Things a practical concept?

If you believe what the likes of LG and Samsung have been promoting this week [in January 2014] at CES [Consumer Electronics Show], everything will soon be smart. We'll be able to send messages to our washing machines, run apps on our fridges, and have TVs as powerful as computers. It may be too late to resist this movement, with smart TVs already firmly entrenched in the mid-to-high-end market, but resist it we should. That's because the "Internet of Things" stands a really good chance of turning into the "Internet of unmaintained, insecure, and dangerously hackable things."

The Problem with the Internet of Things

These devices will inevitably be abandoned by their manufacturers, and the result will be lots of "smart" functionality—fridges that know what we buy and when, TVs that know what shows we watch—all connected to the Internet 24/7, all completely insecure.

While the value of smart watches or washing machines isn't entirely clear, at least some smart devices—I think most notably phones and TVs—make sense. The utility of the smartphone, an Internet-connected computer that fits in your pocket, is obvious. The growth of streaming media services means that your antenna or cable box are no longer the sole source of televisual programming, so TVs that can directly use these streaming services similarly have some appeal.

But these smart features make the devices substantially more complex. Your smart TV is not really a TV so much as an all-in-one computer that runs Android, WebOS, or some custom operating system of the manufacturer's invention. And where once it was purely a device for receiving data over a coax cable, it's now equipped with bidirectional networking interfaces, exposing the Internet to the TV and the TV to the Internet.

The result is a whole lot of exposure to security problems. Even if we assume that these devices ship with no known flaws—a questionable assumption in and of itself if SOHO [small office/home office] routers are anything to judge by—a few months or years down the line, that will no longer be the case. Flaws and insecurities will be uncovered, and the software components of these smart devices will need to be updated to address those problems. They'll need these updates for the lifetime of the device, too. Old software is routinely vulnerable to newly discovered flaws, so there's no point in any reasonable time frame at which it's OK to stop updating the software.

In addition to security, there's also a question of utility. Netflix and Hulu may be hot today, but that may not be the case in five years' time. New services will arrive; old ones will die out. Even if the service lineup remains the same, its underlying technology is unlikely to be static. In the future, Netflix, for example, might want to deprecate old APIs [application program interface] and replace them with new ones: Netflix apps will need to be updated to accommodate the changes. I can envision changes such as replacing the H.264 codec with H.265 (for reduced bandwidth and/or improved picture quality), which would similarly require updated software.

To remain useful, app platforms need up-to-date apps. As such, for your smart device to remain safe, secure, and valuable, it needs a lifetime of software fixes and updates.

A History of Nonexistent Updates

Herein lies the problem, because if there's one thing that companies like Samsung have demonstrated in the past, it's a total unwillingness to provide a lifetime of software fixes and updates. Even smartphones, which are generally assumed to have a two-year life cycle (with replacements driven by cheap or "free" contract-subsidized pricing), rarely receive updates for the full two years (Apple's iPhone being the one notable exception).

A typical smartphone bought today will remain useful and usable for at least three years, but its system software support will tend to dry up after just 18 months.

This isn't surprising, of course. Samsung doesn't make any money from making your two-year-old phone better. Samsung makes its money when you buy a new Samsung phone. Improving the old phones with software updates would cost money, and that tends to limit sales of new phones. For Samsung, it's lose-lose.

Our fridges, cars, and TVs are not even on a two-year replacement cycle. Even if you *do* replace your TV after it's a couple years old, you probably won't throw the old one away. It will just migrate from the living room to the master bedroom, and then from the master bedroom to the kids' room. Likewise, it's rare that a three-year-old car is simply consigned to the scrap heap. It's given away or sold off for a second, third, or fourth "life" as someone else's primary vehicle. Your fridge and washing machine will probably be kept until they blow up or you move houses.

These are all durable goods, kept for the long term without any equivalent to the smartphone carrier subsidy to promote premature replacement. If they're going to be smart, software-powered devices, they're going to need software life cycles that are appropriate to their longevity.

That costs money, it requires a commitment to providing support, and it does little or nothing to promote sales of the latest and greatest devices. In the software world, there are companies that provide this level of support—the Microsofts and IBMs of the world—but it tends to be restricted to companies that have at least one eye on the enterprise market. In the consumer space, you're doing well if you're getting updates and support five years down the line. Consumer software fixes a decade later are rare, especially if there's no system of subscriptions or other recurring payments to monetize the updates.

Of course, the companies building all these products have the perfect solution. Just replace all our stuff every 18–24 months. Fridge no longer getting updated? Not a problem. Just chuck out the still perfectly good fridge you have and buy a new one. This is, after all, the model that they already depend on for smartphones. Of course, it's not really appropriate even to smartphones (a mid/high-end phone bought today will be just fine in three years), much less to stuff that will work well for 10 years.

These devices will be abandoned by their manufacturers, and it's inevitable that they are abandoned long before they cease to be useful.

Superficially, this might seem to be no big deal. Sure, your TV might be insecure, but your NAT [network address translation] router will probably provide adequate protection, and while it wouldn't be tremendously surprising to find that it has some passwords for online services or other personal information on it, TVs are sufficiently diverse that people are unlikely to expend too much effort targeting specific models.

Bringing Planned Obsolescence to Our Durable Goods

But I think the issue is more significant than it might seem. First, I don't think this kind of enforced, premature obsolescence is good for anyone other than hardware companies. Replacing an otherwise perfectly good TV ahead of time just because its Netflix app is stale and no longer maintained is a reprehensible waste of resources. I would like to think that most people would recognize the wastefulness this represents and wouldn't ditch their TV just because its built-in Netflix app is out of date. But I'm confident that such thoughts have entered the minds of TV company executives, and they're hoping people do precisely that. You'll have a TV that works well for a year or two and then *gets worse*. If you sell TVs, that's good news.

Second, not all devices are as trivial as TVs. Cars are increasingly computerized. They're also really insecure in ways that unambiguously compromise safety. Smart cars (as distinct from oh so cute Smart cars), boasting their own Internet connections and rich software platforms, are only going to make this worse. Worse, it doesn't seem that car companies take software security seriously.

So if you want to participate in the Internet of Things, your choice will be to send your perfectly good car to the crusher or let any bored hacker disable your brakes, probably by sending you a text message or something equally insane. The sensible option? Don't participate in the Internet of Things. Take out the SIM, turn off the Bluetooth. Use the perfectly good satnav [satellite navigation] app that your phone has.

I don't want to sound all Luddite [opposed to technological change] here. I got a new TV recently, and it's a smart TV. It's pretty unavoidable if you want a mid-range or better set. I love the idea of all our things being connected to the Internet, of having our media follow us, available and accessible from whatever device we happen to be using (though this only goes so far; I cannot fathom the appeal of smart fridges or washing machines). But a world of hundreds of millions of connected devices, all ignored and abandoned by their manufacturers, is not a healthy one.

As such, there are only two ways in which smart devices make sense. Manufacturers either need to commit to a lifetime of updates, or the devices need to be very cheap so they can be replaced every couple years.

If manufacturers won't commit to providing a lifetime of updates—and again, the experience with smartphones is, I think, instructive here—then these smart devices are a liability. Avoiding them entirely is troublesome, but we can certainly avoid *using them*. Ignore the smarts built into your TV. Don't add your account details to the Netflix app, don't hook them up to your networks, don't show them when the TV boots. Don't stick a SIM into your smart car. Don't play the manufacturer's game.

Instead, use smarts elsewhere. For example, instead of using the smartness in your TV (such that upgrading the smarts means upgrading the entire TV too, pointlessly wasting the LCD), you leave the smarts in a small set-top box like a Roku or an Apple TV. That will give you your streaming media and rich connectivity, but it's in a box that's relatively disposable. Sure, even that box won't be supported forever (though I daresay it will be supported for longer than a smart TV), but replacing it means replacing a small $99 gadget—not a thousand bucks of flat panel.

Periodical and Internet Sources Bibliography

The following articles have been selected to supplement the diverse views presented in this chapter.

Shelley Galasso Bonanno	"Social Media's Impact on Relationships," PsychCentral, April 7, 2015.
Jeffrey Burt	"Internet of Things Is Coming, but Is That Good or Bad?," eWeek, May 14, 2014.
Cody C. Delistraty	"Online Relationships Are Real," *Atlantic*, October 2, 2014.
Eliana Dockterman	"Kim Stolz: How Social Media Is Ruining Our Relationships," *Time*, June 24, 2014.
Michal Brendan Dougherty	"John R. MacArthur Says the Internet Makes Bad Journalism. He Has a Point," *The Week*, August 15, 2014.
Mathew Ingram	"Is the Internet Making Journalism Better or Worse? Yes," Gigaom, July 21, 2011.
Sam Laird	"Is Social Media Destroying Real-World Relationships?," Mashable, June 14, 2012.
J.M. Porup	"The Printing Press Created Journalism. The Internet Will Destroy It," Contributoria, April 2014.
Thomas Ricker	"First Click: You Can't Spell 'Idiot' Without IoT (Internet of Things)," The Verge, May 4, 2015.
Kellie Riordan	"The Internet Can Deliver Better Journalism, Not Just Clickbait," The Conversation, September 2, 2014.
Bruce Schneier	"The Internet of Things Is Wildly Insecure—and Often Unpatchable," *Wired*, January 6, 2014.

OPPOSING
VIEWPOINTS®
SERIES

CHAPTER 3

What Challenges Does the Internet Pose?

Chapter Preface

As the Internet has become a bigger part of everyday life since it first exploded in popularity in the 1990s, various legal, ethical, and social challenges related to its use have arisen. In recent years, the widespread use of social media platforms such as Facebook and Twitter has led to the emergence of cyberbullying among teens and other young Internet users. An online extension of traditional face-to-face bullying that often involves constant or near constant social media harassment through the posting of derogatory messages, cyberbullying can do severe emotional harm and has even led to suicide in some cases. Widespread Internet availability has also made it possible for terrorists to take their activities online and engage in what is now referred to as cyberterrorism. Cyberterrorists may use the Internet to recruit others into their terrorist groups or to attack their enemies through cyberspace. While cyberbullying and cyberterrorism are certainly major concerns, one of the earliest and most hotly debated Internet problems is the issue of online piracy.

Online piracy is the use of the Internet to illegally download songs, movies, software, or other copyrighted materials. Engaging in this sort of piracy has become an increasingly widespread phenomenon in recent years, in part as a consumer reaction to the ever rising costs associated with buying albums or visiting the movie theater. At the same time, governments have generally struggled to effectively adapt existing copyright and intellectual property laws to better protect content producers in cyberspace. As a result, online piracy, though occasionally stymied for brief periods, continues to flourish.

The online piracy problem first started with the advent of the MP3 in the late 1990s. MP3s are a type of compressed audio sound file that allows the file size of a digital recording to be significantly reduced with relatively little loss of sound quality. The small size of MP3s made it possible for people to easily share and download music files online, leading to the creation of peer-to-peer (P2P) file sharing networks. One of the earliest of these networks was Napster, a wildly popular P2P service founded in 1999. Until it was effectively shut down in 2001, millions of people around the world used Napster to illegally download songs, much to the dismay of professional musicians and others in the recording industry. Even after Napster ceased operations, many other P2P networks continued to operate. As Internet connection speeds gradually became faster, users also began illegally downloading movies and other large files through more advanced P2P networks that provide access to torrent files. Torrent files are small files that allow users to locate and download parts of larger files, such as whole movies, from various computers connected to a P2P network.

In an effort to protect the rights of copyright holders and cut down on the monetary losses incurred because of online copyright infringement, the US government has attempted to fight piracy with tougher laws and stricter enforcement. While these efforts have had some measure of success, online piracy continues to be a widespread occurrence.

In the realm of public opinion, views on this kind of piracy are still sharply divided. Of course, most content producers are opposed to piracy because it infringes on their rights and cuts into their profits. Supporters of piracy, on the other hand, allege that piracy is a justifiable means of acquiring content without paying the exorbitant prices charged by producers. Some even argue that piracy is actually beneficial to producers because it provides them with a great deal of free exposure.

The authors of the viewpoints in the following chapter debate the effects of online piracy and discuss other challenges presented by the Internet.

> *"The fact is that digital piracy isn't as harmful as the creative industry wants you to think. . . . It's actually helpful!"*

Online Piracy Is Not Harmful

Jeff Cuellar

In the following viewpoint, Jeff Cuellar argues that the entertainment industry has overstated the threat of online piracy. What is more, he goes on to suggest that piracy has actually been beneficial to the companies responsible for producing the movies, music, and other forms of entertainment currently being pirated online. Cuellar is an author, copywriter, and former US Army intelligence analyst who now writes for MoneySmart, a Singapore-based finance blog.

As you read, consider the following questions:

1. According to Cuellar, what does the financial state of the entertainment industry suggest about the impact of online piracy?

2. Why is piracy important for prospective professionals, according to the viewpoint?

3. According to Cuellar, why is piracy actually advantageous for many companies?

I recently came across an interesting Channel NewsAsia article regarding piracy. No, it wasn't about Somali pirates pulling off raids on commercial shipping along the Horn of Africa. It was about *digital* piracy. According to the survey mentioned in the article, 74% of Singaporeans aged 19–24 actively participate in digital piracy. . . .

That's pretty surprising!

I really thought the numbers would have been *much higher*. The fact that Singaporeans digitally pillage movies, music, and software with Genghis Khan–like tenacity shouldn't surprise anyone. But I'm not condemning them for it. The fact is that digital piracy isn't as harmful as the creative industry *wants* you to think. Hell, it's actually helpful!

Here's why.

Piracy Isn't as Harmful as the Creative Industry Wants You to Believe

Hollywood and the big record labels have launched a crusade against digital piracy under the argument that they're taking "huge" losses, which hurts the average Joe working on the set or in the studio. If you've visited a certain local cinema chain (the one that plays 20 minutes of commercials before finally playing the damn movie), you've seen the anti-piracy public service announcements condemning it.

But is digital piracy *really* causing the entertainment industry such losses?

A recent study conducted by Bart Cammaerts, Robin Mansell, and Bingchun Meng from the London School of Economics and Political Science (LSE) proves otherwise. Here are the interesting facts that the study uncovered:

- *Cinema*: Despite the Motion Picture Association of America's (MPAA's) claim that online piracy is devastating to the movie industry, *Hollywood achieved record-breaking global box office revenues of $35 billion USD [US dollars] in 2012, a 6% increase over 2011.*

- *Music*: Declining sales of recorded music were offset by increasing revenue from live performances and growing digital revenues, including streaming services. In 2012, some 34% of revenue globally (excluding revenue from live performances) was generated by digital channels including streaming and downloads, up from 27% three years earlier. *In addition, worldwide sales of recorded music increased in 2012 for the first time since 1999.*

- *Gaming*: The gaming industry has been generating new income streams very successfully by developing combinations of free advertising models, in-apps buying and micro pricing. *It is projected to grow at 6.5% with estimated revenues of $87 billion USD in 2017, up from $63 billion in 2012.*

- *Publishing*: In 2013, the global book publishing industry was worth some $102 billion USD, larger than the film, music or video games industries. *Although revenues from print book sales have declined, this has been offset by increases in sales of e-books and the rate of growth is not declining despite reports lamenting the "end of the book."*

How much did you spend on "authentic" CDs, DVDs, Blu-ray disks, and books in 2013? Compare that to how much you spent on live performances, "authentic" downloads/digital streaming, and trips to the movie theater in 2013. Do your numbers correlate to the findings of the study above?

Piracy Gives You Access to the Career Tools You Need

If you're a student, musician, or work in the creative industry, then you know that software piracy is about as commonplace as well ... working on a pirate ship. Students need word pro-

The Upside of Piracy

10 years after studios began trying to bring down online file-sharing services, suing their users and arguing that the entertainment industry could collapse, it's clear that their claims were overblown and their tactics counterproductive. Online piracy (which is not even the correct term, as it implies profiteering) hasn't come to destroy consumer entertainment. It is more than likely its savior, an amalgamation of lending library, viral-advertising hub, and market expansion tool.

Jake Rossen, "How Hollywood Can Capitalize on Piracy,"
MIT Technology Review, *October 17, 2013.*

cessing and office programs, musicians need editing software, and of course, "creatives" need image editing and illustration software.

Of course, the biggest reason why people pirate is *price*. Many software packages retail for hundreds or thousands of dollars—money that the working-class student or young professional can't afford. Not yet anyway.

"Software is just too expensive," says Sarah, a young graphic designer working for a local design agency. "It's easy to say an investment of $1,000 in Photoshop CS6 will be returned in just a few projects. But with my tight budget and fierce competition for design services, I really can't afford to wait to save up and buy it."

Piracy isn't just about cost—it's also about economic contribution. Students and young professionals such as Sarah pirate software they *need* in order to build up their professional skills and knowledge. Having experience with certain types of software is key to landing jobs in Singapore's increasingly competitive job atmosphere.

Engineers *need* experience with AutoCAD and Autodesk. Graphic designers *need* experience with Photoshop and InDesign. *That's just the way it is.* And in this unfair world that we live in, the people who break the rules by pirating software to get a leg up on the competition are more valuable to employers. Employers don't want to train job applicants on software. They want candidates who already have experience using required software programs.

Piracy Helps Companies Innovate Products and Services You Will Pay For

Borders and HMV (RIP you lost fragments of my childhood) make up just a small percentage of the long-standing companies that have perished over the last few years. No doubt digital piracy had a hand in their demise, but then again, so did their inability to adapt to the digital age and evolving consumer habits.

Then again, is it really all that surprising? Think about it. How can you compare a store that's selling a Blu-ray for $60 SGD [Singapore dollars] to a peer-to-peer (P2P) sharing site that gives you the same movie for free? That's like matching a young Mike Tyson against some no-name fighter. It's not a contest. It's a massacre.

But several companies have learned enough from digital piracy to change their business models and provide products and services consumers *are willing to pay for*:

- *Netflix*: With 40 million global subscribers and growing, Netflix has succeeded despite piracy because it gives consumers what they want, *"TV shows & movies anytime, anywhere. For one low monthly price."* At least to consumers *outside of Singapore* anyway. . . .

- *Adobe*: The company behind some of the most pirated software programs in the world finally caught on to the piracy problem and did something ingenious. Adobe introduced monthly subscriptions at reasonable prices for students, individuals, and businesses. Now there's less of a need to pay $1,000+ on software that you subscribe to for less than $100 a month.

- *Steam*: While Steam hasn't completely eliminated computer game piracy, it has definitely kept it in check by making digital distribution cheap, easy, and mainstream for gamers. Steam did it by giving video game companies a low-piracy environment for them to offer their games while providing better value, service, and gaming environment for consumers.

- *Sony PlayStation Network*: The PlayStation Network borrows some of Netflix's ingenuity (and even offers Netflix streaming in the U.S.) by letting consumers own or "rent" new or classic movies via download/streaming video. You can also purchase games from the convenience of your home or even join PlayStation Plus for free games, discounts, and online "cloud" game storage. Unfortunately, customers in Singapore aren't given the option to buy/rent movies, or use Netflix.

Final Note: Yes, I think we all agree that piracy is stealing. But to say that piracy is more harmful than good completely neglects many of the positive changes it has brought consumers. The reality is that piracy is here to stay, there's no changing that.

Even if you block sites that enable P2P sharing with a "Great Firewall of China" type of censorship operation, more sites will just pop up and replace them. Mitigating the "danger" of piracy doesn't take government intervention, but innovation on the part of businesses.

As the great Kevin Spacey once said on the subject, "Give users control, what they want, when they want it, at a fair price, and stop worrying about piracy."

> "*Remember that culture doesn't exist in a vacuum—actual, living people create it, and they deserve to make a living just as much as anyone else.*"

Online Piracy Is Economically Harmful

Elmo Keep

In the following viewpoint, Elmo Keep argues that online piracy is detrimental to the entertainment industry and unjustly harmful to those who make their livings as producers of consumable content. She contends that consumers are wrong to selfishly steal content for convenience without giving a thought to the cost of making that content. Keep is an Australian writer and journalist whose work has appeared in the Melbourne Age *and the* Sydney Morning Herald, *as well as online at the Rumpus and the Awl.*

As you read, consider the following questions:

1. According to Keep, why did piracy originally become a problem in Australia?

2. How has piracy been detrimental to the entertainment industry, according to the viewpoint?

Elmo Keep, "Piracy Is About Theft, Not a Lack of Legal Alternatives," Techly.com.au, June 13, 2014. © 2014 Techly. Reproduced by permission.

3. According to Keep, why shouldn't consumers feel entitled to pirate the content they wish to enjoy?

Almost any piece of media you could ever want is available to purchase legally, and yet Australia consistently tops lists of global piracy rates. Why?

Long the digital consumer's clarion cry has been, "If only it were available to buy legally and easily, I would."

This is iterated all the way from consumers up to tech suppliers like Google Australia whose policy representative has publicly claimed that there is "credible evidence emerging that online piracy is primarily an availability and pricing problem."

This logic was originally employed to justify accessing content illegally, a rationalisation of a widespread behaviour. After all, if there was no way to get something you wanted immediately via legal channels, what were you meant to do? *Wait* for the DVDs? Instant gratification—the dominant cultural capital of the Internet—doesn't work like that.

Only we know this vow to pay for things if only it were as simple as torrenting (which is actually not so simple and involves several more steps than most legal services require to ensure access) isn't true. As ways of legally accessing digital content continue to multiply, the number of people in Australia illegally downloading content continues to increase, not fall.

Why?

The Source of Piracy

Some of it may be attributable to the lag times Australians once upon a time had to cope with when waiting to access overseas content, and old habits die hard.

Networks adopted fast-tracking to address this issue, music releases have been on an instant global release schedule for many years, and new books to market are available instantly on e-readers through online marketplaces. All of this made it hard for many to understand why it hadn't always been the case.

However, turning the entire economic models of huge industries like film, television, publishing, music and journalism around on a dime to fit consumer expectation is just not something that is possible to do without eroding the revenues that make the enterprises viable in the first place.

To replace the way in which release schedules had been set up to deliver certain returns with an untested new way (digitally) not guaranteed to make the same money is not good business practise, it's suicide.

The Effect of Piracy

Since the emergence of Napster in 1997, revenues from the global music industry have halved. Labels merged and huge numbers of staff and artists were let go. The industry is still trying to find ways to recover the losses wrought by piracy.

Streaming services are seen as the best way to satisfy consumer demand for immediate and cheap music, but the jury is still out as to if or not the revenue model is strong enough to support itself, with many high-profile artists taking their music out of services like Spotify, citing their deleterious effect on new and emerging artists. These services, though encouraging, do not appear to generate the revenue needed to replace hard goods. However, small revenues are preferable to zero.

As far as consumer behaviour goes, legal alternatives like streaming services are available, offering an enormous amount of culture across all the aforementioned industries at very low prices—prices set not by producers, but by tech sector providers. With very few exceptions, it's somewhat difficult to find something that can't be accessed legally.

In the rare case where that is true, there is always good old-fashioned waiting. Though for many, the loss of social

© Paul Zanetti, "Internet Piracy," Cagle Post, February 4, 2010.

capital in not being able to talk with one's friends about the latest episode of premium American television can be practically lethal, and my heart goes out to them. There are many ways to pay for content, people would just prefer not to when they can get it for free.

The Price of Culture

The fact is, consumers don't set the price for products of culture: creators and producers do. They do because they know what making things actually costs and what revenue is required to make a return on their investment.

It's like any other business—except unlike any other business it is an easy product to take without paying for it. The lay person who just really wants to watch *American Horror Story* right now has little understanding of the business decisions required to make and distribute this TV show locally while ensuring a return on substantial investments.

Without that knowledge, it's easy to subscribe to misinformed rhetoric about piracy, framing it as primarily an availability and pricing problem, not an ingrained behaviour problem aided by easy accessibility to free content.

Unless you are a film producer intimately acquainted with the economics of a production and the balance sheet required to get a film out to audiences, then your opinion doesn't count for much.

Unless you are a publisher who knows exactly what the margins are on signing a new author, supporting their work and creating, marketing and releasing their book to the world, then your opinion doesn't count for much.

Unless you have overseen a local television production and know exactly how much it will cost to pay the number of people needed to make the show, then your opinion doesn't count for much.

Unless you're a record label manager who knows what digital revenues generate and how these changes are affecting their artists, then your opinion doesn't count for much.

Rejecting Piracy

If you aren't a professional in the production industries, working in the commercial sector to actually make the culture that we consume, then you're in no position to make a business decision for someone else.

Let's stop propping up myths about how the economics of the content industries work and instead put our money where our mouths are. If you turned up to work one day only to be told that you won't get paid for your labour from now on, you'd be angry about it too. Remember that culture doesn't exist in a vacuum—actual, living people create it, and they deserve to make a living just as much as anyone else.

> *"The psychological impact [of cyberbullying] can be devastating, and suicide is not unknown among young victims. For some victims, the damage to their sense of dignity and emotional well-being could persist for years."*

Technology Gave Rise to Cyberbullying. Can It Also Stop It?

Jessica Mendoza

Jessica Mendoza is a writer for the Christian Science Monitor. *In the following viewpoint, she reports that several social media networks, including Twitter and Facebook, are taking measures to curb cyberbullying on their sites. Mendoza argues that the effects of online bullying are extremely harmful to children and can persist into young adulthood. She explains that the very technology that made cyberbullying possible is now being used to combat the practice, as several applications have been created that allow kids to report bullying incidents anonymously or record the incident without the bully's knowledge. Mendoza concludes that cyberbullying may be difficult to stop, but efforts must be made to end the harmful practice.*

As you read, consider the following questions:

1. According to Mendoza, how many students surveyed between 2006 and 2014 had experienced cyberbullying?

2. According to *BJPsych Bulletin*, what may victims of cyberbullying experience?

3. According to the viewpoint, what does STOPit allow users to do?

Twitter is stepping up against cyberbullying.

On Tuesday, the social network announced policy changes aimed at promoting safe discourse and interaction for users. The updates, which include a broader definition of violent content and an additional enforcement option against abusers, are the latest in efforts by social networks, tech companies, researchers, and others to put a stop to online abuse and harassment, often using the same kinds of innovations that gave cyberbullying room to grow in the first place.

These efforts provide further support to existing ways of preventing and punishing cyberbullying, including government intervention, school policies, and family monitoring and awareness.

"We believe that users must feel safe on Twitter in order to fully express themselves," according to the social network's blog. "[W]e need to ensure that voices are not silenced because people are afraid to speak up."

Online harassment and cyberbullying have for years given parents, schools, and governments plenty of cause to search for solutions. On average, about a quarter of students surveyed between 2006 and 2014 had experienced cyberbullying—defined as willful and repeated harm via computers, cell phones, and other devices—at some point in their lives, according to the Cyberbullying Research Center.

The Danger of Cyberbullying

Cyberbullying is relational aggression. It is intended to make the victim feel frightened, humiliated, helpless and too often—hopeless. What makes cyberbullying particularly harmful, and in the case of at least five young people who have committed suicide, so deadly is the nature and virulent reach of electronic media.

Suzanne Phillips, "Coping with Cyberbullying:
The Use of Technology to Terrify," PBS.org, 2011.

The psychological impact can be devastating, and suicide is not unknown among young victims. For some victims, the damage to their sense of dignity and emotional well-being could persist for years.

"Victims experience lack of acceptance in their peer groups, which results in loneliness and social isolation," according to a study in the *BJPsych Bulletin*. "The young person's consequent social withdrawal is likely to lead to low self-esteem and depression. . . . The effects of being bullied at school can persist into young adulthood."

The first of Twitter's updates changes the language of its violent threats policy, allowing the platform to intercede even when an abuser is vague about the kind of violence he or she is threatening or promoting. Previously, the policy required the aggressor to post specific threats before Twitter could respond.

Twitter staff will also start locking accounts they regard as abusive for set amounts of time. Users whose accounts have been locked may be required to verify their phone number and delete offensive content before being allowed back in.

"Twitter's mission is to give everyone the power to create and share ideas and information instantly, without barriers,"

Vijaya Gadde, Twitter's general counsel, wrote last week in an op-ed for the *Washington Post*. "It is not our role to be any sort of arbiter of global speech. However, we will take a more active role in ensuring that differences of opinion do not cross the line into harassment."

Other companies have been trying to innovate, as well. Facebook's bullying prevention hub, done in partnership with the Yale Center for Emotional Intelligence, provides a space for teens, parents, and educators to discuss and address cyberbullying. The social network also has a team dedicated to promoting empathy and respect online, the *New York Times* reported last year.

In 2013, one New Jersey–based company created an app called STOPit, which lets kids anonymously report to preselected adults whenever they witness or experience abuse, whether online or off. Today, more than 83 school districts in 13 states use STOPit, according to NJ.com. The program has also ranked among CNN's and the *Washington Post's* top apps that make a difference.

Similar apps include Bully Block, which lets users record incidents of bullying as they happen, without the aggressor knowing; and Bully Box, which, like STOPit, lets users report anonymously and provides access to resources on bully prevention, counseling, and others.

How effective these new tools will be in curbing abuse and cyberbullying have yet to be determined. Challenges are bound to lie ahead, and mistakes will probably be made, Twitter's Ms. Gadde said. But, she added, that should not stop anyone from trying.

"We know that our efforts to protect both the safety of our users and their right to express themselves freely will create tensions that can be difficult to resolve," she wrote for the *Post*. "But those difficulties simply acknowledge the importance of those underlying values. These are tough issues that challenge Twitter and the Internet generally."

> *"Claims by the media and researchers that cyberbullying has increased dramatically and is now the big school bullying problem are largely exaggerated."*

The Cyberbullying Threat Is Overstated

American Psychological Association

In the following viewpoint, the American Psychological Association presents a look at cyberbullying from Norwegian psychologist Dan Olweus. Olweus contends that cyberbullying, though dangerous, does not present as great a risk to children as traditional bullying. He asserts that cyberbullying is effectively overshadowed by traditional bullying, which is a much greater threat to children. The American Psychological Association is the nation's largest organization of psychologists and other psychology experts and professionals.

As you read, consider the following questions:

1. According to the viewpoint, how did Olweus determine that cyberbullying is less prevalent than traditional bullying?

American Psychological Association, "Cyberbullying Less Frequent than Traditional Bullying, According to International Studies," APA.org, August 4, 2012. © 2012 American Psychological Association. Reproduced by permission.

2. According to Olweus, why is it difficult to determine the true effect of cyberbullying?

3. What needs to be done to properly address cyberbullying, according to the viewpoint?

Traditional in-person bullying is far more common than cyberbullying among today's youth and should be the primary focus of prevention programs, according to research findings presented at the American Psychological Association's [APA's] 120th annual convention.

"Claims by the media and researchers that cyberbullying has increased dramatically and is now the big school bullying problem are largely exaggerated," said psychologist Dan Olweus, PhD, of the University of Bergen, Norway. "There is very little scientific support to show that cyberbullying has increased over the past five to six years, and this form of bullying is actually a less frequent phenomenon."

APA presented Olweus at the convention with its 2012 award for distinguished contributions to research in public policy for his 40 years of research and intervention in the area of bullying among youth.

Studies Discredit Cyberbullying Claims

To demonstrate that cyberbullying is less frequent than "traditional" bullying, Olweus cited several large-scale studies he conducted, including one involving approximately 450,000 U.S. students in grades three to 12. In the latter, regular surveys were conducted in connection with the introduction of Olweus's bullying prevention program in 1,349 schools from 2007 to 2010. Another study followed 9,000 students in grades four through 10 in 41 schools in Oslo, Norway, from 2006 to 2010.

In the U.S. sample, an average of 18 percent of students said they had been verbally bullied, while about 5 percent said they had been cyberbullied. About 10 percent said they had

The Overstatement of Cyberbullying

Dan Olweus, a professor of psychology at the University of Bergen in Norway who created one of the most successful bullying prevention programs in the world, has published a controversial paper this year [2012] arguing cyberbullying is much less common than conventional bullying. And there is no evidence it has increased in recent years, he says, despite the escalating use by teens of the Internet and mobile phones. . . .

Mr. Olweus said he recognized that his reality check on cyberbullying, published in the *European Journal of Developmental Psychology*, would create "some turbulence" in academic circles, but he felt it necessary to correct a distorted picture.

"I felt that there were a number of reports about increasing levels [of cyberbullying]: that this was very frequent, that children, as soon as they got this possibility, started doing negative things online," he said. "We had data and they suggest quite a different picture."

Graeme Hamilton,
"Amanda Todd and the Greatly Exaggerated
Cyberbullying Plague: Web Harassment Not on the Rise,
Researcher Says," National Post, October 26, 2012.

bullied others verbally and 3 percent said they had cyberbullied others. Similarly, in the Norwegian sample, 11 percent said they had been verbally bullied, 4 percent reported being the victim of cyberbullying, 4 percent said they had verbally bullied others and 1 percent said they had cyberbullied others.

Other analyses showed that 80 percent to 90 percent of cyberbullied students were also exposed to traditional forms of bullying—that is, they were bullied verbally, physically or in more indirect, relational ways, such as being the subject of false, mean rumors. Similarly, most cyberbullies also bullied in more traditional ways.

All students filled out the Olweus bullying questionnaire, which asks extensive questions about an individual's experience with bullying, both as a victim and a perpetrator. The survey includes questions about the students' experience with cyberbullying, which is defined as taking place via a mobile phone or the Internet.

"These results suggest that the new electronic media have actually created few 'new' victims and bullies," Olweus said. "To be cyberbullied or to cyberbully other students seems to a large extent to be part of a general pattern of bullying where use of electronic media is only one possible form, and, in addition, a form with low prevalence."

Addressing the Crisis

This is not to say that cyberbullying cannot be a problem in schools and outside of school, Olweus noted. Cyberbullied children, like targets of more traditional bullying, often suffer from depression, poor self-esteem, anxiety and even suicidal thoughts, he said.

"However, it is difficult to know to what extent these problems actually are a consequence of cyberbullying itself. As we've found, this is because the great majority of cyberbullied children and youth are also bullied in traditional ways, and it is well documented that victims of traditional bullying suffer from the bad treatment they receive," he said. "Nonetheless, there are some forms of cyberbullying—such as having painful or embarrassing pictures or videos posted—which almost certainly have negative effects. It is therefore important also to take cyberbullying seriously both in research and prevention."

Olweus recommends that schools and communities invest time and technical efforts in anonymously disclosing identified cases of cyberbullying—and then communicating clearly and openly the results to the students. This strategy can substantially increase the perceived risk of disclosure and is likely to reduce further the already low prevalence of cyberbullying, he said.

"Given that traditional bullying is much more prevalent than cyberbullying, it is natural to recommend schools to direct most of their efforts to counteracting traditional bullying. I don't want to trivialize or downplay cyberbullying but I definitely think it is necessary and beneficial to place cyberbullying in proper context and to have a more realistic picture of its prevalence and nature," he said.

Periodical and Internet Sources Bibliography

The following articles have been selected to supplement the diverse views presented in this chapter.

Nick Bilton	"Internet Pirates Will Always Win," *New York Times*, August 4, 2012.
Dan Holden	"Is Cyber-Terrorism the New Normal?," *Wired*, January 2015.
Sharon Jayson	"Studies Show Cyberbullying Concerns Have Been Overstated," *USA Today*, August 4, 2012.
Martin C. Libicki	"Cyberattacks Are a Nuisance, Not Terrorism," *Newsweek*, February 8, 2015.
Craig Offman	"The Problem with the Term 'Cyberbullying,'" *Globe and Mail*, October 18, 2013.
Suzanne Phillips	"Dealing with Cyberbullying: Online and Dangerous," PsychCentral, October 19, 2013.
Mateo Pimentel	"Cyberterrorism: Real Security Threat or Boogeyman?," News Junkie Post, January 26, 2015.
Wayne Scholes	"Piracy's Ripple Effect on the Global Economy," *Diplomatic Courier*, January 14, 2014.
Chase Szakmary	"Cyber Attacks Will Be the Greatest National Security Threat in the 21st Century," PolicyMic, February 6, 2013.
Paul Tassi	"Whatever Happened to the War on Piracy?," *Forbes*, January 24, 2014.
Michele Ybarra	"The Top 5 Myths of Cyberbullying," *Psychology Today*, March 3, 2014.

OPPOSING
VIEWPOINTS®
SERIES

CHAPTER 4

Can the Internet Be Dangerous?

Chapter Preface

Since the Internet has emerged as a major mass communications medium, people have questioned whether its use might have any adverse consequences for those who spend time in cyberspace. Indeed, there are many possible causes for concern in the online world. Among the most fundamental concern, for example, is the issue of whether using the Internet is itself an addictive activity. Proponents of Internet addiction theories argue that people who spend too much time online can actually become psychologically dependent on surfing the web. Others have posited that certain specific online activities, such as Internet gambling, can also become addictive in their own right. Perhaps the most debated Internet danger, however, is what some suggest is posed by the consumption of Internet pornography.

For practically as long as the Internet has existed, it has played host to various pornographic materials. Pornography on the Internet became and remains popular for many of the same reasons it has also persisted in home video and print formats—it allows users to engage with sexually explicit materials in the privacy of their own homes with complete anonymity. The overwhelming demand for pornographic materials online has transformed the Internet into a virtual environment in which practically any variety of pornography, even the most extreme sorts, are readily available at little to no cost or restriction. As a result of this ease of access, pornography is now likely more widely viewed and used than ever before.

The prevalence of Internet pornography today has, in turn, led many people to question the impact that its use has on individuals and society at large. Those who believe that the use of Internet pornography is addictive and potentially dangerous typically argue that pornography affects the brain much the same way that drugs do, leaving users physically and mentally hooked and involuntarily going back for more. Those who fall on the other side of this argument often posit that unhealthy, compulsive consumption of Internet pornography is the result of user irresponsibility and not the material itself or the Internet in general.

Regardless of whether or not using the Internet is in any way harmful, it is certain to remain a large part of everyday life moving forward. As a result, the ongoing debate over the effects of Internet use is sure to continue as well.

The following chapter further examines the effects of online pornography and explores the potential danger of Internet addiction.

> *"A decade of research ... had only proven what the 1997 study had suspected, that the Internet could inspire the same patterns of excessive usage, withdrawal, tolerance, and negative repercussions as more traditional substance use."*

Internet Addiction Is a Legitimate Mental Condition

Maria Konnikova

In the following viewpoint, Maria Konnikova argues that Internet addiction is a legitimate mental condition and should be treated as such. Citing the similarities between the effects of recognized conditions such as gambling addiction and the effects of excessive Internet use, Konnikova asserts that Internet dependence should be classified as an addiction. At the same time, however, she also acknowledges the difficulty of determining when continual Internet usage really is addiction. Konnikova is a New Yorker *contributor who specializes in issues related to science and psychology.*

As you read, consider the following questions:

1. According to Konnikova, why is Internet addiction more complicated than other addictions?

2. According to the viewpoint, why is the categorization of excessive Internet use as an addiction still disputed?

3. According to Konnikova, why is treating Internet addiction more difficult than treating other forms of addiction?

M arc Potenza, a psychiatrist at Yale and the director of the school's Program for Research on Impulsivity and Impulse Control Disorders, has been treating addiction for more than two decades. Early in his career, he, like most others studying addiction at the time, focused on substance abuse problems—cocaine and heroin addicts, alcoholics, and the like. Soon, however, he noticed patients with other problems that were more difficult to classify. There were, for example, the sufferers of trichotillomania, the inescapable urge to pull your hair until it falls out. Others had been committed for problem gambling: They couldn't stop no matter how much debt they had accumulated. It was to this second class of behaviors—at the time, they were not called addictions—that he turned his attention. Were they, he wondered, fundamentally the same?

In some sense, they aren't. A substance affects a person physically in a way that a behavior simply cannot: No matter how severe your trichotillomania, you're not introducing something new to your bloodstream. But, in what may be a more fundamental way, they share much in common. As Potenza and his colleague Robert Leeman point out in a recent review of the last two decades of research, there are many commonalities between those two categories of addiction. Both behavioral and substance addictions are characterized by an inability to control how often or how intensely you engage in an activity, even when you feel the negative consequences. Both come with urges and cravings: You feel a sudden and debilitating need to place a bet or to take a hit in the middle of a meal. Both are marked by an inability to stop.

Substance and behavioral addictions also both seem to have some genetic basis, and, Potenza has found, the genetics seem to share many common characteristics. Some of the same gene mutations found in alcoholics and drug addicts, for instance, are often found in problem gamblers. Furthermore, the neurochemistry that these addictions evoke in the brain is similar. Drugs, for example, are known to affect the mesolimbic dopamine pathway—the pleasure center of the brain. Behaviors like gambling similarly activate the same parts of the brain's reward circuitry. Earlier this year [2014], Trevor Robbins, a cognitive neuroscientist at the University of Cambridge, and the psychologist Luke Clark, then at Cambridge and now the director of the Centre for Gambling Research at the University of British Columbia, came to a similar conclusion after conducting an overview of the existing clinical research into behavior addictions. The basic neuroscience of the two types of addiction showed a substantial overlap.

Internet as Addiction

In recent years, however, Potenza has been increasingly treating a new kind of problem: people who come to him because they can't get off the Internet. In some ways, it seems exactly like the behavioral addictions that he has been treating for years, with much of the same consequences. "There are core features that cut across those conditions," Potenza says. "Things like the motivation to engage in the behaviors and put aside other important elements of life functioning, just to engage in them." Or, in the words of Robbins and Clark, "behavior for behavior's sake."

There's something different, and more complicated, about Internet addiction, though. Unlike gambling or even trichotillomania, it's more difficult to pin down a quantifiable, negative effect of Internet use. With problematic gambling, you're losing money and causing harm to yourself and your loved ones. But what about symptoms like those of a woman I'll call

Sue, who is a patient of Potenza? A young college student, Sue first came to Potenza at the behest of her parents, who were becoming increasingly concerned about the changes in their daughter. A good—and social—student in high school, she found herself depressed, skipping or dropping classes, forego- ing all college extracurricular activities, and, increasingly, us- ing the Internet to set up extreme sexual encounters with people she had never met in real life. Sue spends the majority of her time online social networking, but does that mean that she has a problem with the Internet or with managing her so- cial life and her sex life? What if she were obsessively online, for the rest of her life, but learning languages or editing Wiki- pedia?

The Internet, after all, is a medium, not an activity in and of itself. If you spend your time gambling online, maybe you have a gambling addiction, not an Internet addiction. If you spend your time shopping online, maybe it's a shopping ad- diction. "Some people have posited that the Internet is a ve- hicle and not a target of disorder," Potenza said. Can you be addicted to a longing for virtual connectivity in the same way that you can be addicted to a longing for a drink?

The Problem of Internet Addiction

As far back as 1997, before the days of ubiquitous smart- phones and laptops, when dial-up and AOL [America Online] dominated the landscape, psychologists were already testing the "addictive potential" of the World Wide Web. Even then, certain people were exhibiting the same kinds of symptoms that appeared with other addictions: trouble at work, social isolation, and the inability to cut back. And, to the extent that there was something that people referred to as an addiction, it appeared to be to the medium itself—the feeling of connect- edness to something—rather than to an activity that could be accomplished via that medium.

By 2008, the worry about Internet addiction progressed to such a point that the *American Journal of Psychiatry* published an editorial strongly suggesting that Internet addiction be included in the next, and fifth, version of the so-called bible of psychiatry, the *Diagnostic and Statistical Manual [of Mental Disorders]* (*DSM*). A decade of research, wrote the psychiatrist Jerald Block, had only proven what the 1997 study had suspected, that the Internet could inspire the same patterns of excessive usage, withdrawal, tolerance, and negative repercussions as more traditional substance use. What's more, Block concluded, "Internet addiction is resistant to treatment, entails significant risks, and has high relapse rates." It was a disease that needed treatment as much as any other disease did.

The realization that the Internet may be inducing some addictive-seeming behaviors in its own right has only grown more widespread. One study, published in 2012, of nearly twelve thousand adolescents in eleven European countries, found a 4.4 per cent prevalence of what the authors termed "pathological Internet use" or using the Internet in a way that affected subjects' health and life. That is, through a combination of excessive time spent online and that time interfering with necessary social and professional activities, Internet use would result in either mental distress or clinical impairment, akin to the type of inability to function associated with pathological gambling. For maladaptive Internet use—a milder condition characterized by problematic but not yet fully disruptive behavior—the number was 13.5 per cent. People who exhibited problematic use were also more likely to suffer from other psychological problems, such as depression, anxiety, ADHD [attention-deficit/hyperactivity disorder], and OCD [obsessive-compulsive disorder].

Internet addiction ultimately did not make the list of officially recognized behavioral addictions in *DSM-5*, but compulsive gambling did. It had taken gambling several decades of extensive research to make the cut, and there simply wasn't enough systematic, longitudinal data about Internet addiction. But, to Potenza, Block's conclusions rang true. Sue wasn't the first patient that he'd seen for whom the Internet was causing substantial, escalating problems; that number had been rising slowly over the last few years, and his colleagues were reporting the same uptick. He had been working with addicts for decades, and her problems, as well as those of her fellow sufferers, were every bit as real as those of the gambling addicts. And it wasn't just an iteration of college angst in a new form. It was something endemic to the medium itself. "I think there are people who find it very difficult to tolerate time without using digital technologies like smartphones or other ways of connecting via the Internet," Potenza said. It's the very knowledge of connectivity, or its lack, that's the problem.

He agrees that the subject remains far more disputed than other behavioral areas: Psychiatrists are no longer debating that behavioral addictions exist, but they are ambivalent about whether Internet use can be classified as one of them. The difference, Potenza feels, is one of degree. Internet use remains so disputed because it's changing too rapidly for researchers to keep up, and, though the immediate effects are fairly visible, there's no telling what the condition will look like over the long term.

Finding a Solution

Internet addiction remains a relatively minor part of Potenza's work—he estimates that fewer than ten out of every forty patients he sees come in for an Internet problem. These patients tend to be younger, and there seems to be a gender divide: Male patients are more likely to be addicted to activities like online gaming; women, to things like social networking. But it's hard to make generalizations, because the nature of the problem keeps changing. "The truth is, we don't know what's normal," Potenza says. "It's not like alcohol where we have healthy amounts that we can recommend to people." In other

What Is Internet Addiction?

Internet addiction, otherwise known as computer addiction, online addiction, or Internet addiction disorder (IAD), covers a variety of impulse-control problems, including:

- Cybersex Addiction - compulsive use of Internet pornography, adult chat rooms, or adult fantasy role-play sites impacting negatively on real-life intimate relationships.
- Cyber-Relationship Addiction - addiction to social networking, chat rooms, texting, and messaging to the point where virtual, online friends become more important than real-life relationships with family and friends.
- Net Compulsions - such as compulsive online gaming, gambling, stock trading, or compulsive use of online auction sites such as eBay, often resulting in financial and job-related problems.
- Information Overload - compulsive web surfing or database searching, leading to lower work productivity and less social interaction with family and friends.
- Computer Addiction - obsessive playing of off-line computer games, such as Solitaire or Minesweeper, or obsessive computer programming.

"Internet and Computer Addiction,"
HelpGuide.org, April 2015.

words, just because you're online all day doesn't mean you're an addict: There are no norms or hard numbers that could tell us either way.

Behavioral addictions are quite real, and, in a number of respects, Internet addiction shares their core features. But the differences that set it apart mean that the avenues of treatment may differ somewhat from those typically associated with behavioral—and substance—addictions. One of the most effective ways of treating those addictions is by identifying and removing the catalysts. Cancel the credit card. Get rid of the bottles. Avoid the places you go to drink or to gamble, and, at times, avoid the people you do these activities with. Be aware of your triggers. With the Internet, though, that solution is far more problematic. Computers and virtual connections have become an integral part of daily life. You can't just pull the plug and expect to function. A student may be suffering from what she's doing online, but she also might need to use the Internet for her classes. The thing she needs to avoid in order to do well is also the thing she needs to use to reach the same end.

But Potenza hopes that that very ubiquity can, ultimately, be enlisted as part of the solution. You may not be able to remove the triggers, but you can reprogram the thing itself, a kind of virtual bottle that automatically clamps shut when you've had too much to drink or a casino that turns off its lights as you move into dangerous territory. "The hope is to harness these same technologies within the mental-health field to promote health," Potenza said. Already, there are apps that block certain web pages or that disable a computer's Internet connectivity. There are also ones that tell you when to put your smartphone away. Why not customize them, in conjunction with a therapist, to avoid the pitfalls that are most likely to lead to problem use for you personally? As is so often the case, technology may end up being both the problem and the answer.

"Your Internet addiction isn't an addiction but the logical extension of existing biological functions, not necessarily a sign of dysfunction."

We Are All Internet Addicts Now—Just Don't Call It That

Jared Keller

In the following viewpoint, Jared Keller argues that Internet addiction is not a legitimate medical condition. Instead, he contends that excessive or compulsive Internet use is actually a biological function of sorts. Keller is a New York–based journalist whose work has appeared in such publications as the Atlantic, Bloomberg Businessweek, *and the* Los Angeles Review of Books.

As you read, consider the following questions:

1. According to the viewpoint, why do people spend so much time online?

2. Why does excessive Internet use not rise to the level of other legitimate compulsions, according to the viewpoint?

3. According to Keller, when does excessive Internet use become a legitimate concern?

Having trouble shutting down your computer? Can't stop refreshing your Facebook and Twitter streams? Did you close Reddit in your browser window . . . only to open Reddit right back up again? If you're concerned that your Internet use is becoming a compulsion, you're probably right: New research suggests that our uncontrollable desire to click may be deeply rooted in human evolution.

"The Internet is not addictive in the same way as pharmacological substances are," cognitive scientist Tom Stafford at the University of Sheffield in the U.K. told Tia Ghose at Live-Science. "But it's compulsive; it's compelling; it's distracting."

As Stafford explains, our love for the Internet is rooted in the fact that human beings, in Ghose's words, "compulsively seek unpredictable payoffs." The cognitive-reward structure offered by services like e-mail and social media are similar to those of a casino slot machine: "Most of it is junk, but every so often, you hit the jackpot." This is a symptom of low-risk/high-reward activities like lotteries in general.

As researchers found in a 2001 article in *International Gambling Studies,* systems that offer a low-cost chance of winning a very large prize are more likely to attract repetitive participation and, in turn, stimulate excessive (and potentially problematic) play. Although the stimuli are different (the payoff on the Internet being juicy morsels of information and entertainment rather than money), Stafford says that the immediacy and ubiquity of Internet "play"—i.e., being able to check your tweets or e-mails on your phone with no major transaction cost—only increases the likelihood that someone will get sucked into a continuous cycle.

"The web's unpredictable payoffs train people much in the same way Ivan Pavlov trained dogs," Ghose writes. "Over time, people link a cue (e.g., an instant-message ping or the Facebook home page) with a pleasurable rush of feel-good brain chemicals. People become habituated to seek that social rush over and over again."

The message of Stafford's research is clear: Your brain really wants you to click on all of those cat photos. "The next time you wonder whether you're spending too much time on Facebook or BuzzFeed or whatever, just remind yourself: You're wasting time because your brain wants you to," writes my former colleague Megan Garber at the *Atlantic*. "The Internet's charisma is a function not just of all the great stuff that lives on it, but also of humans' carefully honed survival mechanisms—mechanisms evolved long ago, in response to vicious enemies. We can't quit our cat videos, it turns out, because of . . . lions."

Anyone who spends a significant amount of time on the Internet, whether for work or pleasure, can see the tendrils of Stafford's research in their day-to-day behavior. I often find myself cycling between my Gmail inbox, Facebook, Twitter, and other services, especially social media services which are designed to constantly refresh automatically or allow users to "infinitely scroll" through the contents of their feeds. And as Internet access and usage increases, this trend is likely to grow. According to the Pew Internet and American Life Project, 81 percent of American adults use the Internet as of survey, with 74 percent of users going online "just for fun or to pass the time." A 2011 Ipsos media poll found that the amount of time "affluent" Americans in general spend online rose about 20 percent from 2010 to more than 30 hours weekly; affluent Millennials spend more than 40 hours a week online, "essentially a full-time job."

Does this mean we're all Internet addicts now? Yes and no. Using the *DSM* [*Diagnostic and Statistical Manual of Mental Disorders*] as a guide, Dr. Kimberly Young at the Center for Internet Addiction defines "Internet addiction" as an impulsive-control problem with four distinct subtypes: cyber-

Internet Addiction Is Not Real

For most people, the tie to the Internet, however powerful and consuming, brings much more pleasure or productivity than pain and impairment. This is more love affair and/or tool using than enslavement and is not best considered the stuff of mental disorder. It would be silly to define as psychiatric illness behavior that has now become so much a necessary part of everyone's daily life and work.

Allen J. Frances,
"Internet Addiction: The Next New Fad Diagnosis,"
Psychology Today, *August 13, 2012.*

sexual addiction (Internet pornography), cyber-affair/relational addiction (an addiction to chat rooms and other online social forums), net compulsions (addictions to online gaming, online gambling, and eBay), and information overload (an addiction to database searches). The tipping point for Internet "addiction" is its impact on your day-to-day activities.

01. Do you feel preoccupied with the Internet (think about previous online activity or anticipate next online session)?

02. Do you feel the need to use the Internet with increasing amounts of time in order to achieve satisfaction?

03. Have you repeatedly made unsuccessful efforts to control, cut back, or stop Internet use?

04. Do you feel restless, moody, depressed, or irritable when attempting to cut down or stop Internet use?

05. Do you stay online longer than originally intended?

06. Have you jeopardized or risked the loss of significant relationship, job, educational, or career opportunity because of the Internet?

07. Have you lied to family members, therapists, or others to conceal the extent of involvement with the Internet?

08. Do you use the Internet as a way of escaping from problems or of relieving a dysphoric mood (e.g., feelings of helplessness, guilt, anxiety, depression)?

According to Young, answering "yes" to five or more questions may mean you suffer from Internet addiction.

However, "addiction" in the descriptive sense does not mean "addiction" in the clinical sense. Whether "Internet addiction" should be regarded as a serious psychological illness has been a matter of debate for years; the creators of the *DSM-5* considered relegating Internet addiction to a section on behavioral disorders along with sex and gambling addictions, but opted to list it as a "condition for further study" instead of recognizing it as an official disorder. That Stafford places compulsive Internet surfing in the same cognitive category as gambling and other low-risk/high-reward activities defined as behavioral rather than purely psychological problems by the *DSM* suggests that your Internet fixation, however severe or uncontrollable it may seem, likely doesn't reach the level of other compulsions. (It's worth noting here that "Internet addiction disorder" was originally proposed as a satirical hoax by Dr. Ivan Goldberg in 1995, based on the *DSM*'s description of pathological gambling, in an effort to parody how psychiatry's bible categorizes excessive behavior.)

"Lots of us are furtively checking e-mails in movie theaters and in the middle of the night, feel lost when temporarily separated from our electronic friends, and spend every spare minute surfing, texting, or playing games. But does this really qualify us as addicts?" asked Dr. Allen Frances, former chair of the DSM-IV Task Force, in *Psychology Today*. "No, not usually. Not unless our attachment is compulsive and without reward or utility; interferes with participation and success in real life; and causes significant distress or impairment. For most people, the tie to the Internet, however powerful and consuming, brings much more pleasure or productivity than pain and impairment."

More plainly put: Your Internet addiction isn't an addiction but the logical extension of existing biological functions, not necessarily a sign of dysfunction. So when does your Twitter fixation move from simply being a symptom of how humans cognitively interface with the Internet (and an annoyance to your friends and family) to something more? If you find yourself totally incapable of leaving the house to go to work, or to do anything but move between infinite browser windows, don't tweet about it; instead, consider calling a doctor.

"*More akin to cocaine than to books or public speeches, Internet pornography is not the sort of 'speech' the First Amendment was meant to protect from government censorship.*"

Online Pornography Is Harmful

Morgan Bennett

In the following viewpoint, Morgan Bennett argues that Internet pornography is dangerously addictive. Citing various studies and statistics, Bennett paints Internet pornography as the equivalent of a drug to which people can become easily addicted—even to the point of serious psychological harm. This leads her to conclude that Internet pornography should be prohibited. Bennett, a graduate of Pepperdine University School of Law and Belmont University, is a writer whose work has appeared on websites and blogs such as Public Discourse *and* Ethika Politika.

As you read, consider the following questions:

1. According to Bennett, what makes Internet pornography different from other forms of pornography?

Morgan Bennett, "The New Narcotic," ThePublicDiscourse.com, October 9, 2013. © 2013 Public Discourse. Reproduced by permission.

2. Why is Internet pornography addictive, according to the viewpoint?

3. According to Bennett, why is the addictiveness of Internet pornography worse than the addictiveness of real drugs?

The other day, I overheard a guy say that Starbucks was "the greatest drug dealer in the United States." Being a guilty party to that sort of "drug dealing," I'll recuse myself from discussing the merits of such a charge.

But what if I told you that *the Internet* is the greatest drug dealer in the United States?

The Challenge of Internet Pornography

A growing body of research supports such an assertion as it relates to a new "narcotic": Internet pornography. The National Survey on Drug Use and Health estimated that in 2008 there were 1.9 million cocaine users. According to the Central Intelligence Agency [CIA], there are an estimated 2 million heroin users in the United States, with some 600,000 to 800,000 considered hard-core addicts. Compare these numbers to the *40 million* regular users of online pornography in America.

Neurological research has revealed that the effect of Internet pornography on the human brain is just as potent—if not more so—than addictive chemical substances such as cocaine or heroin. In a statement before Congress, Dr. Jeffrey Satinover, a psychiatrist, psychoanalyst, physicist, and former fellow in psychiatry at Yale, cautioned:

With the advent of the computer, the delivery system for this addictive stimulus [Internet pornography] has become nearly resistance-free. It is as though we have devised a form of heroin 100 times more powerful than before, usable in the privacy of one's own home and injected directly to the

brain through the eyes. It's now available in unlimited supply via a self-replicating distribution network, glorified as
art and protected by the Constitution.

Though pornography, in one form or another, has been
around for most of human history, its content and the way
people access and consume it have drastically changed in the
past few decades with the advent of the Internet and related
technologies.

There are three main reasons *Internet* pornography is radically different from earlier forms: its (1) affordability (K.
Doran, assistant professor of economics at Notre Dame University, estimates that 80% to 90% of porn users view free
content online); (2) accessibility (24/7 access anywhere with
an Internet connection); and—most importantly—(3) anonymity. Those three factors combined with Internet
pornography's experiential depiction of real people perform-
ing real sex acts while the viewer observes has created a potent
narcotic—in the most literal sense.

Yet many would argue that pornography is merely
"speech," a form of sexual "expression" that should be protected as a constitutional right under the First Amendment.

The question of First Amendment rights is undeniably the
ultimate hurdle to clear from a legal standpoint—and I take
up that question in tomorrow's *Public Discourse* essay. Today I
begin my analysis from a scientific perspective, because recent
neurological findings have exposed Internet pornography to
be something much, much more than mere "speech."

Internet Pornography: The New Narcotic

While the term "drug addiction" typically has been reserved
for chemical substances physically ingested (or inhaled or
injected) into the body, Internet pornography—taken in
through the eyes—affects the brain chemically and physically
in a manner similar to that of illegal chemical substances. William M. Struthers, professor of psychology at Wheaton Col-

lege, explains in his book *Wired for Intimacy: How Pornography Hijacks the Male Brain* that pornography works "through the same neural circuit, has the same effects with respect to tolerance and withdrawal, and has every other hallmark of an addiction."

This is because the same parts of the brain react to both illegal substances and sexual arousal. Dopamine, the chemical triggered by sexual arousal and orgasm, is also the chemical that triggers addiction pathways in the brain. As Donald L. Hilton Jr., MD, a practicing neurosurgeon and a clinical associate professor of neurosurgery at the University of Texas, observes:

> Pornography is a visual pheromone, a powerful 100-billion-dollar-per-year brain drug that is changing sexuality even more rapidly through the cyber-acceleration of the Internet. It is "inhibiting orientation" and "disrupting premating communication between the sexes by permeating the atmosphere."

Think of the brain as a forest where trails are worn down by hikers who walk along the same path over and over again, day after day. The exposure to pornographic images creates similar neural pathways that, over time, become more and more "well-paved" as they are repeatedly traveled with each exposure to pornography. Those neurological pathways eventually become *the* trail in the brain's forest by which sexual interactions are routed. Thus, a pornography user has "unknowingly created a neurological circuit" that makes his or her default perspective toward sexual matters ruled by the norms and expectations of pornography.

These "brain trails" are able to be initiated and "paved" because of the *plasticity* of brain tissue. Norman Doidge, MD—a psychiatrist, psychoanalyst, and author of the *New York Times* and international best seller *The Brain That Changes Itself*—explores the impact of neuroplasticity on sexual attraction in an essay in *The Social Costs of Pornography*. Dr. Doidge notes that brain tissue involved with sexual preferences (i.e., what "turns us on") is especially malleable. Thus, outside stimuli—like pornographic images—that link previously unrelated things (e.g., physical torture and sexual arousal) can cause previously unrelated neurons within the brain to learn to "fire" in tandem so that the next time around, physical torture actually *does* trigger sexual arousal in the brain. This in-tandem firing of neurons creates "links" or associations that result in powerful new brain pathways that remain even after the instigating outside stimuli are taken away.

Internet Pornography as Addiction

In light of the new brain science, the relevant scientific com-munity (the American Society of Addiction Medicine), which used to believe addiction was primarily a *behavior*, recently re-defined "addiction" as primarily a *brain disease* revolving around the neurological rewards system. Internet pornography's powerful force on the neurological reward sys-tem clearly places it within this new definition of "addiction."

Some might argue that many substances and activities—such as TV, food, shopping, etc.—can cause addiction-forming chemicals in the brain, yet we certainly don't want the govern-ment regulating how much TV we watch, how often we shop, or how much we eat. While there are plenty of people with addictions to TV, food, and shopping, Dr. Hilton argues that sexual images are "unique among natural rewards" because sexual rewards, unlike food or other natural rewards, cause "persistent change in synaptic plasticity." In other words, In-ternet pornography does *more* than just spike the level of do-pamine in the brain for a pleasure sensation. It literally *changes the physical matter* within the brain so that new neurological pathways *require* pornographic material in order to trigger the desired reward sensation.

So how does Internet pornography compare with illegal addictive chemical substances like cocaine or heroin? Cocaine

Addiction to Internet Pornography

Pornography addiction and the Internet have always been natural partners in crime. The Internet provides the privacy that makes such an addiction possible, as well as the widespread availability and volume of content that may help to fuel obsessive behavior.

"Addiction to Internet Pornography,"
HypersexualDisorders.com, June 15, 2012.

is considered a stimulant that increases dopamine levels in the brain. Dopamine is the primary neurotransmitter that most addictive substances release, as it causes a "high" and a subsequent craving for a repetition of the high, rather than a subsequent feeling of satisfaction by way of endorphins. Heroin, on the other hand, is an opiate, which has a relaxing effect. Both drugs trigger chemical tolerance, which requires higher quantities of the drug to be used each time to achieve the same intensity of effect.

Pornography, by both arousing (the "high" effect via dopamine) and causing an orgasm (the "release" effect via opiates), is a type of polydrug that triggers both types of addictive brain chemicals in one punch, enhancing its addictive propensity as well as its power to instigate a pattern of increasing tolerance. Tolerance in pornography's case requires not necessarily greater quantities of pornography but more *novel* pornographic content like more taboo sexual acts, child pornography, or sadomasochistic pornography.

The Chemistry of Internet Pornography

Sexual arousal is the result of testosterone, dopamine, and norepinephrine surges, whereas the transcendence and euphoria experienced during orgasm are related to the release of endogenous opiates. While pornography activates the appetitive system by way of dopamine, an orgasm caused by pornography does *not* release endorphins, which are the chemicals that make us feel satisfied. By contrast, endorphins *are* released after an orgasm caused by having sex with a real human being. This lack of satisfaction, combined with the brain's competitive plasticity, causes the brain to require more and more novel and extreme images to get the same chemical result as before.

While the addictive effects of Internet pornography are similar to a combination of addictive chemical substances, Internet pornography's effects go *beyond* those of chemical substances.

For instance, "mirror neurons" in the brain enable us to learn by watching a behavior and copying it. Professor Struthers writes that, because of mirror neurons, "Viewing a pornographic [video] creates a neurological experience whereby a person vicariously participates in what he is watching." This uniquely interactive addiction is enabled by the combination of stimuli upon both the brain and the body; in Struthers' words, porn use "involves the visual system (looking at porn), the motor system (masturbating), the sensory system (genital stimulation), and neurological effects of arousal and orgasm (sexual euphoria from chemical opiates like addictive dopamine in the nucleus accumbens and reduced fear in the amygdala)."

Another aspect of pornography addiction that surpasses the addictive and harmful characteristics of chemical substance abuse is its permanence. While substances can be metabolized out of the body, pornographic images cannot be metabolized out of the brain because pornographic images are stored in the brain's memory. While substance abusers may cause permanent harm to their bodies or brains from drug use, the substance itself does not remain in the body after it has metabolized out of the body. But with pornography, there is no time frame of abstinence that can erase the pornographic "reels" of images in the brain that can continue to fuel the addictive cycle.

The Truth About Internet Pornography

In sum, brain research confirms the critical fact that pornography is a drug delivery system that has a distinct and powerful effect upon the human brain and nervous system. More akin to cocaine than to books or public speeches, Internet pornography is not the sort of "speech" the First Amendment was meant to protect from government censorship. . . . Those who read books or listen to ideas can use their conscious minds to reason through the assertions and information. But, as Dr. Doidge puts it, "Those who use [pornography] have no sense to the extent to which their brains are reshaped by it." Indeed, they have no idea that pornography is developing "new maps in their brains."

"Porn can affect people, but it does not take them over or override their values."

Online Pornography Itself Is Not Harmful

David J. Ley

In the following viewpoint, David J. Ley argues that Internet pornography is not inherently addictive or harmful. Dismissing many commonly held beliefs about pornography and addiction, Ley contends that viewing pornography is completely safe as long as one does so responsibly. In short, he says that the so-called dangers of online pornography are brought on by the user, not the product itself. Ley is an Albuquerque-based clinical psychologist and an expert in sexuality who has written several books, including Insatiable Wives *and* The Myth of Sex Addiction.

As you read, consider the following questions:

1. According to Ley, how is pornography good for society?

2. What do most people who identify as sex addicts have in common, according to the viewpoint?

3. According to Ley, what can people do to overcome their perceived sexual obsessions?

Porn is not addictive. Sex is not addictive. The ideas of porn and sex addiction are pop psychology concepts that seem to make sense, but have no legitimate scientific basis. For decades, these concepts have flourished in America, but have consistently been rejected by medicine and mental health. The media and American society have accepted that sex and porn are addictive, because it seems intuitively true—we all feel like sometimes, we might do something stupid or self-destructive, when sex is involved. But, this false belief is dangerous, and ultimately not helpful. Because when people buy into the belief that porn is addictive, it changes the argument, and all of a sudden, it seems like it is porn and sex that are the problems. Porn addiction becomes a label, and seems to be an explanation, when in fact, it is just meaningless words and platitudes that distract from the real issue. But sex and porn aren't the problems. You are.

The Effect of Pornography

People do have a strong response to video pornography. Internet porn is very good at triggering male sexuality. The economic forces of the open market have driven modern Internet porn to be very, very effective at triggering male sexual buttons, to get them aroused. But women actually have a stronger physiological response to porn than men and based upon this research, women should be more addicted to pornography than men. But the overwhelming majority of the stories we hear about are men. Why is this? Because one part of this issue is an attack on aspects of male sexuality, including masturbation and use of pornography, behaviors which society fears and doesn't understand.

Porn can affect people, but it does not take them over or override their values. If someone watches porn showing something they find distasteful, it has no impact on their behavior or desires. But, if someone watches porn depicting acts that they, the watcher, are neutral about, then it does make it slightly more likely that they express interest in trying that act themselves. Take anal sex for instance. If a porn viewer finds it disgusting, watching anal pornography isn't going to change that. But, if they are neutral on it, then watching anal porn probably will slightly increase the chance that they would be willing to at least give it a try. But, there is the crux of the issue—the people who gravitate towards unhealthy, violent porn, are people who already have a disposition toward violence. So—the problem is not in the porn, but in those people. Regulating porn access really is going to have no impact on these people as they can (and do) find far more violent and graphic images in mainstream Hollywood films like *Saw*.

The Science of Pornography

Here's some often-ignored empirical science about porn—as societies have increased their access to porn, rates of sex crimes, including exhibitionism, rape and child abuse, have gone down. Across the world, and in America, as men have increased ability to view Internet erotica, sex crimes go down. Believe it or not—porn is good for society. This is correlational data, but it is extremely robust, repeated research. But, it is not a message that many people want to hear. Individuals may not like porn, but our society loves it, and benefits from it.

It is getting increasingly difficult to find men in our society who've never viewed pornography. But, if porn were the problem—if porn were addictive, then the problems of porn would be far, far greater than they are. In fact, in recent studies, fewer than 1% of people report that they have had problems in their life due to difficulties controlling their sexual behaviors, including watching porn. Now—higher numbers, around 10%, report "feeling" that their sexual desires are hard to control, but it is very different to feel something, versus ACTUALLY being out of control.

So—if you are one of that 1%, then what's going on? If it isn't the porn, then it must be you. Something about you (more than one thing, usually) has led you to be a person who makes bad decisions about sex. Now in that, you're not alone—it is in fact a universal truth that people tend to make poorer decisions when they're turned on, whether it's choosing not to wear a condom, or choosing to masturbate to porn when you shouldn't. Call it "sex-goggles," and recognize that human sexual arousal affects our decision making.

But, there's more than that going on for you, if you've decided that porn is your problem. Here's some more real science that suggests some of the things that are going on for you—you like sex. Wow—earth-shattering, right? But several empirical studies have found that self-identified porn addicts tend to be people with high libidos. You are also a person who can get turned on very quickly (when you choose to). Further, you might have grown up in a home (or culture) where sex and masturbation were seen as morally wrong.

Having a high libido is not a bad thing. In fact, one of the things I often argue is that men (and women) who like sex have changed this world, and made it better. Rock stars, politicians, military leaders and sports stars often tend to be people with high libidos, and a high desire to succeed. Sometimes, they actually want to succeed, just so they can have lots of sex.

But, if you are a man who likes sex, and likes porn, is that something you've ever really owned? I'm sad to say that our society has not taught men how to identify and negotiate their sexual desires or needs. We treat sex like a dirty secret. Then, when men get caught, they feed into that dirty secret mentality, and treat sex like it's the problem.

Responsibility Is Key

Those other men, who like sex, watch porn, and don't get in trouble—how do they do that? One thing is that they understand themselves, and their desires. Sometimes, they sit down

Porn Addiction?

Many have attempted to generalize the patterns related to problem substance use to explain other behavior problems, including use of [visual sexual stimuli] (VSS). Surprisingly, a clear, falsifiable theoretical model of "porn addiction" has yet to be described. Some use addiction interchangeably with other labels such as hypersexual disorder (HD)—also known as sexual addiction. Others define addiction broadly to refer to any substance or behavior with evidence of excessive appetite: "appetitive behaviour is excessive, at least in the statistical sense." Simply because a behavior is appetitive and frequently engaged does not mean the behavior is a problem, let alone an addiction.

David Ley, Nicole Prause, and Peter Finn,
"The Emperor Has No Clothes:
A Review of the 'Pornography Addiction' Model,"
Current Sexual Health Reports, *January 2013.*

with their wives and girlfriends and have a real, open discussion about their use of porn, their interest in it, and what it means, and doesn't mean, about their attraction to and interest in their partner. That's a hard, scary discussion (and not one for the first date, please), because it requires a man to stand up for himself and his sexual desires, to be willing to negotiate for those needs, to be willing to compromise, but stay true to himself, while asking for the same in return.

Another thing about those guys, who don't get in trouble for watching porn? They are paying attention to themselves, and they are doing the work that is needed to make good decisions. Some men have the Internet or cable turned off in their hotel rooms, or install a net nanny on their own computer, so they have less temptation. That's not because porn is the problem, but because these men are recognizing (when they're not turned on), that they need to do the prep work, in advance, to make good decisions. It's okay to admit that you make poor decisions when sex or porn are involved—you're not alone in that, and it's not a sin.

But, the responsibility is on you to identify why and how you make bad decisions, and take steps to make better decisions in the future. When you blame the problems on porn, you're telling yourself "porn is more powerful than I am." And I'm here to tell you, that's not true—you CAN take responsibility for your life, your sex, for your good decisions and your bad ones, and have the life you want. Porn's not the problem—you are. But you know what? You're also the solution.

Periodical and Internet Sources Bibliography

The following articles have been selected to supplement the diverse views presented in this chapter.

Morgan Bennett	"The Social & Cultural Poverty of Pornography: When the New Narcotic Shapes Society," *Ethika Politika*, November 10, 2014.
Tony Dokoupil	"Is the Internet Making Us Crazy? What the New Research Says," *Newsweek*, July 9, 2012.
Lauren Dubinsky	"What I Wish I'd Known Before Watching Porn," *Huffington Post*, July 23, 2012.
Allen Frances	"Internet Addiction: The Next New Fad Diagnosis," *Psychology Today*, August 13, 2012.
Alan Henry	"Is Internet Addiction a Real Thing?," Lifehacker, March 25, 2015.
George Pataki and James Thackston	"Online Gambling a Bigger Risk than You Think: Column," *USA Today*, January 30, 2014.
Tom Porter	"Violent Video Games and Online Pornography Leading to Crisis in Masculinity, Warns Psychologist," *International Business Times*, May 10, 2015.
Matt Rousu	"It's Time for the Federal Government to Legalize Internet Gambling," *Forbes*, June 25, 2013.
Venkat Srinivasan	"Internet Addiction: Real or Virtual Reality?," *Scientific American*, May 15, 2014.
Nathan Vardi	"How Wall Street Money Transformed Online Gambling Forever," *Forbes*, August 17, 2015.
Alice G. Walton	"Internet Addiction: The New Mental Health Disorder?," *Forbes*, October 2, 2012.

For Further Discussion

Chapter 1

1. David Rothkopf asserts that Internet access should be considered a basic human right, while Simon Breheny contends that such an interpretation would be flawed and inappropriate. In your opinion, which author makes a better argument? Why?

2. James L. Gattuso argues that net neutrality is detrimental to online freedom. On what evidence does he base his claims? Do you agree with him? Why, or why not?

3. Peter Roff says that global Internet governance would pose a serious threat to the future of the open Internet. Why does he think this is so? Do you think his concerns are legitimate? Why, or why not?

Chapter 2

1. Mathew Ingram and David Sessions express very different opinions on the relationship between the Internet and journalism. With whom do you agree more, and why? Explain.

2. Do you think that Evan Wade's description of himself as a "lover of most anything with processing power" taints the way he views the impact of the Internet of Things? Why, or why not? Do you think the connectivity of things through the Internet will have a positive or negative outcome? Explain your reasoning.

3. Peter Bright argues that the Internet of Things will be impractical, shortsighted, and even wasteful. What evidence does he offer in support of this point of view? Do you think his point is valid? Why, or why not?

Chapter 3

1. Jeff Cuellar contends that piracy is actually beneficial for the entertainment industry, while Elmo Keep asserts that it is harmful. In your opinion, which author presents a more compelling and persuasive argument? Why?

2. According to the American Psychological Association, the fact that cyberbullying is less common than traditional bullying indicates that cyberbullying is not a serious problem. Do you think this is a reasonable conclusion? Why, or why not?

Chapter 4

1. Jared Keller contends that while using the Internet can become a compulsive activity, it cannot be accurately described as addictive. Do you agree with his assessment? Explain your reasoning.

2. David J. Ley argues that Internet pornography is not addictive. What evidence does he offer in support of his argument? Do you think the evidence he presents is sufficient to confirm his conclusion? Explain your answer.

Organizations to Contact

The editors have compiled the following list of organizations concerned with the issues debated in this book. The descriptions are derived from materials provided by the organizations. All have publications or information available for interested readers. The list was compiled on the date of publication of the present volume; the information provided here may change. Be aware that many organizations take several weeks or longer to respond to inquiries, so allow as much time as possible.

Brookings Institution
1775 Massachusetts Avenue NW, Washington, DC   20036
(202) 797-6000
e-mail: communication@brookings.edu
website: www.brookings.edu

Founded in 1927, the Brookings Institution is a sociopolitical think tank that conducts specialized research in foreign policy, Internet policy, government, economics, and other fields. Brookings publishes policy papers such as "Digital Divide: Improving Internet Access in the Developing World Through Affordable Services and Diverse Content" and articles such as "The Power of Convening in Our Digital World." Its print publications include its Policy Briefs series and the quarterly *Brookings Review*.

Federal Communications Commission (FCC)
445 Twelfth Street SW, Washington, DC   20554
1-888-225-5322
website: www.fcc.gov

The Federal Communications Commission (FCC) is a government agency tasked with regulating television, radio, Internet, wire, cable, and satellite communications in the United States. Overseen by Congress, the FCC is responsible for creating and enforcing communications law. As part of its operations, the agency regularly publishes reports such as "Measuring Broadband America—2014" and blog posts such as "The Process of Governance: The FCC & the Open Internet Order."

Fight for the Future

PO Box 55071 #95005, Boston, MA   02205
e-mail: team@fightforthefuture.org
website: www.fightforthefuture.org

Fight for the Future is a nonprofit organization that aims to protect the Internet and encourage its evolution as a tool for the common good. As part of its efforts, Fight for the Future stands against any and all attempts, whether by governments or other entities, to place limitations or restrictions on the Internet that violate the basic rights and freedoms of Internet users. In short, the organization seeks to ensure that people everywhere have affordable Internet access that is unfettered by political interference and respectful of their right to privacy. Its website offers a section with links to articles relevant to the Internet.

Freedom House

1850 M Street NW, Floor 11, Washington, DC   20036
(202) 296-5101 • fax: (202) 293-2840
e-mail: info@freedomhouse.org
website: freedomhouse.org

Freedom House is an independent watchdog organization that works to encourage the spread of freedom worldwide. Through analysis, advocacy, and action, Freedom House seeks to affect positive policy changes that promote the establishment and maintenance of crucial freedoms in countries around the globe. Among the causes for which this organization fights is the spread of Internet freedom, which it supports through its Global Internet Freedom Program. Freedom House's publications include the flagship *Freedom in the World* and reports such as *Freedom on the Net 2014*.

Internet Association

1100 H Street NW, Suite 1020, Washington, DC   20005
e-mail: contact@internetassociation.org
website: internetassociation.org

The Internet Association is a coalition of major online businesses that works to advance policy solutions that protect Internet freedoms, encourage continued innovation and economic advancement, and give users a voice in the Internet's development. Among the high-profile businesses that make up the Internet Association are Amazon, Facebook, Google, Netflix, Twitter, and PayPal.

Internet Corporation for Assigned Names and Numbers (ICANN)

12025 Waterfront Drive, Suite 300
Los Angeles, CA   90094-2536
(310) 301-5800 • fax: (310) 823-8649
website: www.icann.org

The Internet Corporation for Assigned Names and Numbers (ICANN) is a nonprofit public-benefit corporation that works to ensure the Internet continues operating stably and securely at all times. In large part, ICANN fulfills its mission by regulating Internet infrastructure through its administration of the domain name system. Beyond that, ICANN also fulfills its mission by creating and promoting policy that upholds the principles upon which the Internet was founded. ICANN maintains an active blog that features articles such as "Celebrating the Rise of the Modern Internet: The First Dot Com Domain Name Turns 30" and "Working Together to Overcome E-Friction."

Internet Governance Project (IGP)

iSchool@Syracuse University, Syracuse, NY   13244
(315) 443-5616
e-mail: info@internetgovernance.org
website: www.internetgovernance.org

The Internet Governance Project (IGP) specializes in global Internet policy analysis and Internet resource management in hopes of shaping future policy choices. IGP also plays an active role in Internet governance organizations such as ICANN, the United Nations Internet Governance Forum, and the Organisation for Economic Co-operation and Development (OECD). As part of its ongoing policy analysis efforts, IGP regularly releases publications such as "Sovereignty, National Security, and Internet Governance: Proceedings of a Workshop" and "Finding a Formula for Brazil: Representation and Legitimacy in Internet Governance."

Internet Society

1775 Wiehle Avenue, Suite 201, Reston, VA   20190-5108
(703) 439-2120 • fax: (703) 326-9881
e-mail: isoc@isoc.org
website: www.internetsociety.org

The Internet Society is a global organization that works to ensure that the Internet will continue to develop as an empowering open platform for the exchange of ideas. Founded in 1992, the Internet Society specializes in three main areas: standards, public policy, and education. Supported by more than sixty-five thousand members spread out among one hundred chapters worldwide, the Internet Society seeks to facilitate change through the application of its collective technological and communications expertise. As part of its efforts, the Internet Society produces an array of publications, including reports such as "Collaborative Security: An Approach to Tackling Internet Security Issues" and "The Open Internet: What It Is, and How to Avoid Mistaking It for Something Else."

National Science Foundation (NSF)

4201 Wilson Boulevard, Arlington, VA   22230
(703) 292-5111
website: www.nsf.gov

The National Science Foundation (NSF) is an independent federal agency that has been working to promote scientific advancement, health, welfare, and prosperity since it was founded in 1950. It accomplishes this goal by providing funding for research conducted at American universities and colleges. In the early 1980s, the NSF played an instrumental role in the development of the modern Internet when it helped to establish the Computer Science Network (CSNET). Today, the NSF continues to support Internet development through various programs and publications such as "The Internet: Changing the Way We Communicate."

National Telecommunications & Information Administration (NTIA)
Herbert C. Hoover Building (HCHB)
US Department of Commerce, 1401 Constitution Avenue NW
Washington, DC 20230
(202) 482-2000
website: www.ntia.doc.gov

The National Telecommunications & Information Administration (NTIA) is an executive branch government agency located inside the Department of Commerce that is responsible for advising the president on policy issues related to telecommunications and information. Outside of that responsibility, NTIA sponsors a variety of programs aimed at expanding broadband Internet access and ensuring that the Internet remains a free and open medium for innovation and the exchange of ideas. In the course of its operations, NTIA produces numerous publications, including reports such as "Broadband Availability in the Workplace and Exploring the Digital Nation: America's Emerging Online Experience."

Bibliography of Books

Adrian Athique   *Digital Media and Society: An Introduction*. Malden, MA: Polity Press, 2013.

Dana D. Bagwell   *An Open Internet for All: Free Speech and Network Neutrality*. El Paso, TX: LFB Scholarly Publishing, 2012.

Roy Balleste   *Internet Governance: Origins, Current Issues, and Future Possibilities*. Lanham, MD: Rowman & Littlefield, 2015.

Andrew Blum   *Tubes: A Journey to the Center of the Internet*. New York: HarperCollins, 2012.

danah boyd   *It's Complicated: The Social Lives of Networked Teens*. New Haven, CT: Yale University Press, 2014.

Thomas M. Chen, Lee Jarvis, and Stuart Macdonald, eds.   *Cyberterrorism: Understanding, Assessment, and Response*. New York: Springer, 2014.

Laura DeNardis   *The Global War for Internet Governance*. New Haven, CT: Yale University Press, 2014.

Sally Gainsbury   *Internet Gambling: Current Research Findings and Implications*. New York: Springer, 2012.

Mark Graham and William H. Dutton, eds. *Society and the Internet: How Networks of Information and Communication Are Changing Our Lives.* New York: Oxford University Press, 2014.

Samuel Greengard *The Internet of Things.* Cambridge, MA: MIT Press, 2015.

Shane Harris *@War: The Rise of the Military-Internet Complex.* New York: Houghton Mifflin Harcourt, 2014.

Sameer K. Hinduja and Justin W. Patchin *Bullying Beyond the Schoolyard: Preventing and Responding to Cyberbullying.* Thousand Oaks, CA: Corwin, 2015.

Philip N. Howard *Pax Technica: How the Internet of Things May Set Us Free or Lock Us Up.* New Haven, CT: Yale University Press, 2015.

Andrew Keen *The Internet Is Not the Answer.* New York: Atlantic Monthly Press, 2015.

Robin M. Kowalski, Susan P. Limber, and Patricia W. Agatston *Cyberbullying: Bullying in the Digital Age.* West Sussex, UK: John Wiley & Sons, 2012.

Rebecca MacKinnon *Consent of the Networked: The Worldwide Struggle for Internet Freedom.* New York: Basic Books, 2012.

Christian Montag and Martin Reuter, eds. — *Internet Addiction: Neuroscientific Approaches and Therapeutical Interventions.* New York: Springer, 2015.

Lee Rainie and Barry Wellman — *Networked: The New Social Operating System.* Cambridge, MA: MIT Press, 2014.

P.W. Singer and Allan Friedman — *Cybersecurity and Cyberwar: What Everyone Needs to Know.* New York: Oxford University Press, 2014.

Aram Sinnreich — *The Piracy Crusade: How the Music Industry's War on Sharing Destroys Markets and Erodes Civil Liberties.* Boston: University of Massachusetts Press, 2013.

Zack Stiegler, ed. — *Regulating the Web: Network Neutrality and the Fate of the Open Internet.* Lanham, MD: Lexington Books, 2013.

Jose van Dijck — *The Culture of Connectivity: A Critical History of Social Media.* New York: Oxford University Press, 2013.

Gary Wilson — *Your Brain on Porn: Internet Pornography and the Emerging Science of Addiction.* Margate, Kent, UK: Commonwealth Publishing, 2015.

Bob Zelnick and Eva Zelnick — *The Illusion of Net Neutrality: Political Alarmism, Regulatory Creep, and the Real Threat to Internet Freedom.* Stanford, CA: Hoover Institution Press, 2013.

Index

Blodget, Henry, 73–74
Book publishing industry, 104
Brain, and addiction, 128, 135–
136, 141–142, 142–147
Breheny, Simon, 26–30
Bright, Peter, 91–97
Bully Block and Bully Box (apps),
116
Bullying, 117, 119–120, 121
See also Cyberbullying
Bush, George W., 45
BuzzFeed, 72, 73

C

Cable monopolies, 38, 41
Cammaerts, Bart, 103–104
Cars, 96
Castells, Manuel, 14
Censorship
potential, global Internet gov-
ernance, 64–65
protection and human rights,
23
Cerf, Vint, 23
Chambers, John, 37
Chile, 40
Citizen-led journalism, 79
Clark, Luke, 128
"Clickbait," 80, 82
Cocaine, 141, 144–145, 147
Cognitive rewards, 135–136, 141–
142, 143, 144–147
Comcast
blocking, 37, 41, 51–52
cable monopolies, 41
Level 3 (service provider)
conflict, 50–52
net neutrality cases, 32–33, 43,
44, 47, 48

Common carrier classification,
34–35, 43–44, 47–48, 49
Communications Act (1934), 34,
43–44
Compulsive use of the Internet.
See Addiction, Internet
Congress of the United States
communications regulation
and net neutrality, 34, 43–
45, 55, 56
global Internet governance
policy suggestions, 65
Connectivity, devices and gadgets,
84, 86–90, 91–97
Consumer choices
available without net neutrality, 46, 47, 52, 53, 54, 56
net neutrality values, 41–42,
49–50
subscription and rental services, 106–107
Contracts, Internet service providers, 38
Copyright infringement, 100, 101
Creative arts software, 104–106,
106–107
Cuellar, Jeff, 102–107
Current events news coverage,
78–79
Cyber-attacks and warfare
cyberterrorism, 100
potential dangers, global Internet governance, 65
Cyberbullying, 100
effects on victims, 113, 115,
120
methods to curb, 113, 114–
116, 120–121
threat is overstated, 117–121

R

S

CPSIA information can be obtained
at www.ICGtesting.com
Printed in the USA
FFOW05n0729151215